50.

6/99

For Nicole on her Graduation

" Keep going; never stoop; sit tight;
Read something luminous at night. "

— Edmund Wilson

Love,
George

REALMS OF ART

General Editor: PROFESSOR D. TALBOT RICE

1.   *Icons*
2.   *The Transformation of Eros* (*amoretti* and *putti*)
3.   *Stained Glass Windows*
4.   *Mary Icons*
5.   *Mediæval Miniatures*

THE TRANSFORMATION
OF EROS

JOSEF KUNSTMANN

Translated by
M. von HERZFELD

AND

R. GAZE

OLIVER & BOYD
EDINBURGH AND LONDON

OLIVER AND BOYD LTD
Tweeddale Court
Edinburgh 1

39a Welbeck Street
London W.1

A translation of *Ewige Kinder*
published by Buch–Kunstverlag Ettal

First English Edition 1964

Plates printed by H. Weixler, Oberammergau
Text by Oliver and Boyd Ltd, Edinburgh

CONTENTS

1. *Introduction* 7

2. *Notes* 37

3. *Descriptions of Drawings and Plates* ... 51

4. *Acknowledgments* 74

INTRODUCTION

THIS is a picture book, showing angels in the shape of children. They are
certainly some of the most charming things any artist could ever have
produced. One would have thought that they could arouse nothing but
delight. Yet, surprisingly, the winged children give offence to many serious
Christians, who see in them an improper endeavour to prettify the exalted
realms of the spirit. War is declared on the hosts of angel-children in the baroque
churches, and the right to exist denied to them. Of course, no extensive campaign
has been organised against them; it is thought enough just to belittle them and
ridicule them. Frits Lugt for instance writes in an essay on the iconography of
angels (Note 1): "We are quite ready to ignore without regret the swarms

of the lively winged boys, the *putti* of the Italian Renaissance, the everyday found-lings of Greek and Roman art, which are completely foreign to the sacred books of the Bible. With their love of play they have even stolen into the greatest works of architecture; we can only smile contemptuously at them."

But ought we not to ask whether it is possible thus simply to "ignore" the angel-children of the Renaissance and the Baroque? Imagine a baroque altar or the baroque frescoes in a cupola without these children—and the artistic and organic unity of the whole work of art falls to pieces. In most baroque buildings the angel-children outnumber all other figures. And can "love of play" (Note 2) enter the Christian church only by stealth? Surely its home is there, surely it has a right of place within the sacred building? Let Paulinus of Nola (Note 3) give the answer; he provided both stimulus and rules for the pictures to be used in the world of early Christianity. He wrote in his Carmen XIV:

Ferte Deo, pueri, laudem, pia solvite vota,
Et pariter chastis date carmina festa choreis,
Spargite flore solum, praetexite limina sertis.

Children, praise the Lord in your songs, fulfil your pious vows, and taking part in chaste dances offer festive songs; strew the ground with flowers and decorate the gates with garlands.

With these lines the venerable witness to ancient Christian tradition exhorts the Christians to a sacred form of play as we see it represented by Donatello a thousand years later. On the latter's singers' gallery in Florence and his pulpit at Prato, terrestrial and celestial children dance and sing together, just as Paulinus wanted them to do. We know that the saintly bishop's verses refer to a feast at the grave of Felix the Martyr. On the eve of such festivals the faithful used to meet at the tombs of the martyrs and there took part in a love-feast and also performed sacred dances. They had taken over this custom from pre-Christian times, and this was done neither by chance nor through error. On the contrary, this sacred play came to them as a legitimate heirloom. For they shared with the Greeks and the Romans the belief that all human fate, even that of heroes and saints, was a plaything in the hands of God. The Apocrypha as well as Plato's Dialogues express this belief. Gregory of Nazianzus (Note 4) expatiates upon it:

"The lofty Logos plays. He decorated the cosmos at will with colourful pictures."

Maximus Confessor (Note 5), Gregory's disciple, follows the same line:

"We ourselves, begotten and born now like other beings on earth, are thus turned into children and eventually carried from youth into the wrinkles of old age; we resemble the flower which likewise lasts one moment only, then dies and is conveyed to that other life—verily, we deserve to be called a plaything of God."

One has to remember this when one is looking at the gay crowds of *putti* (Note 6). A puritan cannot do justice to them: anyone who wants to understand them must be, or at least try to be, what the Greeks called an *aner spoudogeloios*, that is an earnest-gay man, as far removed from the laughter of the fool as from the brutish seriousness of the Philistine; a man who can smile even when weeping. He will sense a deeper meaning in the playfulness of the *putti* and therefore gladly follow up their origin and history.

It cannot be denied that the early history of *putti* begins in Greek and Roman antiquity. The earliest of these ancestors, flapping their wings, represented the Greek god of love. They were called *erotes*. To understand them we must enquire into the character of the god Eros (Note 7).

Eros is certainly one of the oldest gods of Greece, though Homer does not mention him. The first traces of him are to be found in Hesiod (Note 8); there he belongs to the three primal beings, out of which the world was formed, Gala—Chaos—Eros, earth—primordial matter—love. He has no parents and no connection with any other gods. All that we are told about him is that he creates living seeds. Hesiod further reports that this god of procreation was venerated in Boeotia in a strange shape, namely that of an unhewn stone column (Note 9). But this same author calls him also "the most beautiful of the immortal gods, who loosens the limbs and restrains the temper of all men and gods, but who also overthrows wise counsel." Homer had no use for this god, who could not be fitted into the great family of gods. This difficulty remained to a greater or lesser extent throughout Greek and Roman mythological poetry. Sometimes Aphrodite-Venus (Note 10) was named as his mother, sometimes Artemis-Diana (Note 11). Ares-Mars (Note 12) and Hermes-Mercurius (Note 13) are both suggested as his father. In classical times he is given human shape. Apparently Praxiteles (Note 14) created his prototype, but it has not survived. All later artists took it as their model. They show him as an *ephebe*, as a youth just attaining puberty. Right from the beginning he is almost invariably represented with wings. This indicates that he belongs to the category of "daemons." These were beings flying to and fro between the world and the sky, the lower and the upper regions; they connected what was above with what was below. Winged beings like these were common to the civilisations of the East and the West alike—to the Greeks, the Persians, Babylonians, and Egyptians.

From the very earliest times Eros dominated gods and men, not with normal weapons, but with a flower or a lyre held in his hand. Throughout the ages fertility symbols—the hare, the duck or the goose—were added to his figure. Euripides (Note 15) was the first to put a bow and arrow in his hands, the weapons of Diana, his putative mother. But he always uses them for play, not for war. As he sends forth his arrows, those whom he hits sigh and yet thank him. As art progresses the pranks of this youth become more daring; he dices with his mother Aphrodite for the spoils of love, frolics with swans and dolphins, rides on rams, panthers, and lions—the beasts of Dionysus. Eventually in later allegorical representations he balances the symbols of world domination in his hands—the sphere, the wheel of fire, or a figure of Nike the Greek goddess of victory.

The idea of love ripened psychologically and philosophically at the same time as the development of these forms of representation, and it soon became evident that love can differ widely from love. Euripides had already discovered a lofty and a base Eros (Note 16). The Orphic sect (Note 17) venerated Eros as the creator of the world. For Plato (Note 18) he was the "desire to create in beauty." At the same time love's power spread among men as call and response, as magnanimity and violence, as courting and prostitution. In the Hellenistic era (Note 19) this vastly multiplied power eventually pervaded every province of everyday life. It is therefore not surprising that the figure of the god underwent changes as well. We may now find side by side the orgiastic revelry of Dionysus' *amoretti* with the Paniskes (Note 20), and the exquisite fairy tale of Amor and Psyche by Apuleius (Note 21).

Ovid (Note 22) and Lucian (Note 23) indulged in doubtful jests with the youth. At the same time, however, Virgil (Note 24) was solemnly acknowledging love's all-conquering power with the magnificent verses:

Amor vincit omnia et nos cedamus amori.

The god of love in his manifold shapes could no longer be conceived in the singular. One therefore began to speak of *erotes-amorini* and later on of *amoretti* instead of Eros-Amor. In late antiquity the *erotes* accompanied men and gods throughout their lives; they possessed a kind of omnipresence. They served to light up the wedding night, but also with lowered torch to accompany the soul to the underworld. Love in fact prevailed not in life alone but in death too. The Greeks therefore joined love and death in one world: *eros-thanatos*. The *erotes* are to be found throughout the seasons; they make the flower wreath of spring and tread the grapes in autumn; they bustle about in Vulcan's forge and among the slaves working in cloth-mills; they sail on the high seas and go hunting

merrily; they watch over the sleep of young lovers and provide old age with crutches. The *erotes* combine the most unlikely contrasts and hold together body and soul, heaven, earth, and the underworld.

Yet another evolution went hand in hand with this one. The *erotes* were continuously growing younger. Though the figure of a youth was retained for the representation of sexual love, his merry playing caused the god of love to be personified in the figure of a child. Even in archaic times the poets spoke of his child-like character. Alkman (Note 25) sang: "It is not Aphrodite, it is the roguish Eros who plays these naughty pranks, walking like a child over the heads of flowers! Do not touch them, these tender grasses." However, the child did not seem worthy of representation so far as archaic and classical artists were concerned: for them life began with the epoch of youth. The feeling of pleasure at the sight of a child's body, and the urge to make an image of it, awoke only in the Hellenistic era and in Etruscan art which depended on it. The child-like Eros made his first appearance during that epoch.

The Christians of the first centuries (Note 26) found themselves a part of this "erotic" world of antiquity, and the excavations of Herculaneum and Pompeii illustrate its nature: there is not a living-room, not a garden, hardly a bath or grave without playing *erotes* (Plates 26, 27). How was it possible for Christians to live in this world? We wonder again and again why the Christians of the first centuries did not reject the ancient gods straight away. They made distinctions. They completely accepted some of the figures in the mythology of the ancient world: Orpheus the singer, Hermes-Mercurius the shepherd, Helios-Sol the god of light, only replacing the old name by a new one: Christ the True Light of the world, the Good Shepherd, the Conqueror of the nether-world. Other ancient gods were rejected—Dionysus-Bacchus and Aphrodite-Venus, for example. This principle of selection is of special interest with regard to the *erotes*.

13

We know of no instance in the whole of Christian archaeology where a devotional picture of Eros was taken over from pre-Christian times, not even a representation of the adolescent Eros. We find only child-*erotes* (Plate 8) in the catacombs and in other early places of Christian devotion. And we know of no *putto* in these surroundings accompanied by Aphrodite or Bacchus, nor of any of them indulging in innocent love-play. Only rarely do we meet child-*erotes* playing at games such as dicing, hunting, racing with chariots or riding dolphins (Plates 3, 25, 26).

By contrast we repeatedly find on the walls of the catacombs or on sarcophagi representations of the ancient vintage-feast (Note 27). All the space available for painting is covered with festoons of vines (Plate 9). Crowds of *erotes* climb about among them, pick grapes, collect them in tubs, carry them to the wine-press, and tread them by dancing. The Good Shepherd, resembling the figure of Hermes, often stands in the middle of the scene. This shows what meaning the artist and the patron of the new faith wished to give to these themes, or how they made use of or interpreted existing representations. They had heard the words of Jesus: "I am the vine, ye are the branches" (John, 15,5). And who may they be, the child-like servants, who endeavour to bring about a mystical union between Christ and the church? We find, if not an answer to this question, yet an intimation of it in the Junius Bassus sarcophagus of the Vatican collections. There we see in two reliefs opposed to each other a vintage and a corn harvest. *Erotes* are busy in both, bringing in the fruit. They recall Christ's words that angels will be sent out on the day of judgment to bring the harvest into the barn of the heavenly Father. Another sarcophagus at San Lorenzo Fuori le Mura in Rome shows *erotes* picking flowers. Here a very old Eros-motif is combined with the beliefs of the earliest Christians. The first Greek *erotes* carry a flower, the symbol of life, in their hand. This motif is used in a great variety of forms throughout

Graeco-Roman antiquity. At the time of Augustus it is combined with the representation of the four seasons: Eros picks the flowers of spring, and Christian funereal art saw in these a pledge of the eternal life after death. We see this "earnest money" in the hands of blessed children. Who are these children according to Christian concepts?

There are a number of representations in Christian art of tombs, which take us even closer to the character of these "baptised" Eros-children. In heathen times sarcophagi often had in the centre a circle, looking like a shield and therefore called a *clipeus*, showing the portrait of the dead man or of the husband and wife entombed there. This *clipeus* is held upwards by two children, usually hovering, and according to archaeology these are not *erotes* but *genii*. The Romans believed that every man had a male guardian spirit called *genius*, every woman a female one called *juno*. These guardian spirits accompany the soul entrusted to them throughout life, and lift it after the death of their *protégé* into the circle of heaven, which is symbolised by the round *clipeus*. The Greek concept of the *erotes* and the Roman one of the *genii* were so closely connected—certainly as early as the era of Augustus—that according to the findings of recent research (Note 28) one can say that the Greek idea of the *erotes* was merged in the era of the Roman emperors with the concept of the *genii*.

The Christians found no difficulty in accepting literally the idea of figures like these, for they shared with the whole world of antiquity the belief in guardian spirits which accompanied a man throughout his life and led his soul to the next world after death. Proof of this is afforded by the prayers for the dying and the funeral rites, some of which can be traced right back to the time of the catacombs. One cannot help admiring the early Christians for not having hesitated to give the shape of children to these angels. They thus consecrated an ancient symbol of eternal youth to the lofty spirits, who, according to the word of

Christ, gaze for ever and ever on the face of the heavenly Father. At the same time they endeavoured to relieve death of its most cruel terror.

Once a connection has been established between *erotes* and angels, it is easier to understand several other motifs of the "baptised" *erotes*. We know some ancient sarcophagi (Plate 2) taken into Christian use, which show *putti* playing with hoops and balls (Note 29). Already in the pre-Christian era one of the highest aspirations of the mysteries was hidden in these merry games. When Eros was shown on a Greek vase throwing a hoop or a ball to a maiden, the thinking person recognised even in those days in this hoop or ball the symbol of the sphere of heaven. Things terrestrial—being limited—were at that time represented by a square. Eros therefore throws to the terrestrial maiden a heavenly fate. It is strange that this motif is found again in baroque art. In a poem by the blessed Kreszentia Höss of Kaufbeuren (1682–1744) the Child Jesus plays with a ball, symbolising the human soul. Even in the nineteenth century a similar vision recurs once more in the memoirs of Little Theresia of the Child Jesus (1873–1897). In the Vatican collections there are several *fonde-d'oro* glasses and ivory caskets which are shown to be Christian by the words "Live in Christ" inscribed on them. They are loving-cups and love-caskets, and bear portraits of husband and wife, who lean towards each other, while *amoretti* place wreaths on their heads. In early Christian times loving couples evidently believed that friendly spirits would serve and protect their union.

The most impressive venture of early Christianity, however, was the transformation of the pagan legend of Eros and Psyche into a Christian symbol (Plate 5). The great archaeologist M. Collington (Note 30) explains it as follows: "A sarcophagus in the Lateran shows Eros and Psyche among small *genii* busy with the vintage. Remembering the meaning the Christians gave to the symbol of the vineyard, one cannot fail to see in this scene an allusion to the blessedness of the life to come, where the soul sinks in the ecstasy of the possession of Jesus Christ."

After such a promising connection between ancient and Christian types in the picture of eros-children one might have expected to find a rapid development of the theme of the little angels of love in early Christian and mediaeval art. Strangely enough, however, the *erotes* suddenly almost disappear towards the end of the fifth and early in the sixth century. It is surprising to read in a letter written by St. Nilus to Olympiadorus (Note 31) that the *putti* belonged to an insignificant and good-for-nothing tradition and ought to be suppressed. What is behind this change? First of all, probably the development of Byzantine art. The eastern Christians saw in the imperial court of Constantinople a prototype for their religious concepts. The angels surrounding the throne of the Lord were turned into dignified court officials wearing sumptuous garments stiff with gold, standing without movement, doing nothing except singing the *trisagion* (the thrice holy).

Obviously there was no room there for merrily playing children, but there is a further and stronger reason for the dying out of the *putti*: the background of the earliest Christian mosaics was greyish-white—the colour of the real world around us. Later on preference was given to a blue background, according to ancient colour-symbolism the colour of the starry sky, of the vast cosmos, in which our tangible world hovers or swims. In the fifth century, however, a golden background became usual in the mosaic compositions, and it remained nearly a thousand years as the normal background for all religious images. Gold is the colour of the sphere of fire beyond the world of man's experience. In this absolute beyond the *putto* certainly seemed "insignificant and good-for-nothing"; his play no longer served to unite heaven and earth as it had done originally. The earth had been excluded from the world of images; it no longer deserved to be represented.

In addition there is another and still more deeply founded reason for the disappearance of the *putti*. This is the new concept of that which had given the *erotes* and *amoretti* their name—Love. The Greeks and Romans had already used two different names for it: *Eros-Amor* and *Agape-Caritas*; now a yet sharper distinction was made between the two kinds of love. St. Paul had paved the way, and the mediaeval monks, as they rose to greater influence, elaborated this contrast, stating that there was a divine and celestial love *Agape-Caritas*, and a terrestrial, worldly (indeed, all too worldly) love, which was called *Eros-Amor*. This brought the *erotes* into bad repute; they were looked upon as young sinners or blind fools. They were still known in the Middle Ages in works of mythology (Note 32) and the pictures and sculptures of Antiquity that survived, but image and myth were given a different meaning. Eventually they were made into beings such as those represented by Giotto in the lower church of San Francesco at Assisi: there the great artist symbolised the vow of chastity by the heroic figure of a holy woman; at her side stands a little Amor, now no longer with the victor's band in his hair, but with a bandage over his eyes (Plate 40). This is supposed to signify that worldly love makes blind, while chastity, that is celestial love, alone sees farther. A similar disparagement is to be found in the frescoes of the Campo Santo at Pisa. An unknown artist painted *amoretti* dancing in high spirits; the figure of death towers above them as a warning against these vanities. And later on in history one finds these poor children here and there under the ends of a choir-stall, high up as a gargoyle, or on the capital of a pillar; they are associated with all kinds of questionable and grotesque creatures which belong to the world under rather than above the earth.

This situation remained unchanged for nearly a thousand years. This period might be termed the "thousand years of angels" (Note 33), but they are the ceremonious angels of Santa Maria Maggiore in Rome, San Vitale in Ravenna, San Marco in Venice, San Marco in Florence and the Arena chapel of Padua. There was no room there for jests and play! Not a word about terrestrial love, about *eros* and *amore*!

Only at the end of the thirteenth century did a change occur, when Dante appeared on the scene. He brought the "sweet style" to perfection in Italy and professed that the source of his art was love. "I listen to the breath of love and meditate; I observe what it says to me and write it down; I do not think out anything myself." Dante refused to call his love *caritas*; for him it was very definitely *amore*. By this he understood in the first instance his love for Beatrice, which is in its early stages not to be looked upon as purely spiritual love. He loved passionately and knew the abyss of greed and faithlessness, but he gradually surged above all base feelings and pursued the upward path of his *Divina Commedia*. It is characteristic of his epoch that he personified active spiritual forces in his poem. *Amore* therefore stands as a third person between Dante and Beatrice.

One sonnet of the *Vita Nuova* (1295) describes Amore sitting at Dante's bedside and comforting him in his loneliness with the promise that he will be united to his "Donna Angelica." The figure of Amore is there described with the same words as those used for the youth at the tomb of the Lord in St. Mark's report on the resurrection. Dante felt entitled to think of love as of an angel; for to him it became the all-uniting force, which led him not only to her whom he had chosen above all women, but with her to paradise and to the divine glory. Dante's exalted idea of love, therefore, was related to the wonderful figures that Giotto painted, though it cannot be proved that any connection existed between the spheres of art of these two great contemporaries.

In spite of his lofty conception of the angel of love, however, Dante did not forget the *amoretto*. We read in the eighth sonnet of the *Vita Nuova*:

"I behold you, lady, wearing a fair garland, yourself gentle as a flower, and above I behold flying in haste a sweet angel of love all lowly; and in his mystic song he said: Whoso shall behold me, will praise my lord."

(Translation by P. H. Wickstead, Temple Classics 1906)

Dante, then, knew the exalted figure called Amore, but also his sweet little servant, the *amoretto*. Indeed, Dante seems to have been the first to vindicate as a Christian consciously and explicitly the little love-angel. He thereby summed up a thousand years of early Christian history and handed down to the following centuries the authority to represent the child-like angel of love.

It is not Dante's fault that his successors failed to develop this concept in his

high-minded way. Giovanni Boccaccio (Note 34) still thought of Amore as beautiful and lofty, and even ascribed to him in his *Visione Amorosa* an angel-like face. Yet following all too closely the concept of antiquity, he equipped him with bow and arrow, and encouraged thereby his relapse into paganism. Petrarch (Note 35), in his *Trionfo d'Amore*, hands over without reserve the sceptre to the child. The time had become ripe for the creation of an artistic form for the *putto* of the early Renaissance.

The century seemed to have been waiting for it. German artists had already—quite independently of the tradition of antiquity—made the angels in their altar pictures look younger and younger, until Our Lady in Lochner's pictures appeared surrounded by a host of child-musicians. The acolytes of the later medi-aeval centuries seem to have acted as models for these angel-children. They are now always clothed, and nothing points to a connection with the world of Eros; in fact they seem to be sexless. In Italy, at the beginning of the fifteenth century, one finds a *putto* here and there amidst the *palmetti* and arabesques of the door frames (Note 36). These winged boys are "copied," together with the ornaments, from antique works; as yet they have no life of their own.

The real creator of the Renaissance *putto* was Donatello (Note 37). He breathed life into him. The year 1433 may be called the birth year of the *putto* in modern times. That year Donatello started on the singers' pulpit for the cathedral in Florence (*the cantoria*, now in the museum of the cathedral workshop), and on the exterior pulpit for the cathedral in Prato. In both cases he spread the reliefs on box-like foundations, certainly influenced by reliefs on antique sarcophagi. It seems likely that some themes too were taken over from Antiquity together with the basis of the composition. Yet there was also something basically new here. Donatello showed children as singers, dancers, and musicians, full of a passionate rapture (Plate 13), and so managed to put before our eyes the loftiest form of musical dance: the creature revealing itself to its creator, who is looking on (Note 38). Heaven and earth embrace each other in this dance. What had been lost with the end of Antiquity had now been found again: the loving contact between things terrestrial and things eternal. This was achieved in the dance of the *putto*. From then on the *putto* retained the liveliness of a dancer. Whether sitting, standing, or lying, he likes to lift one foot in a dance; this is one of the characteristics he owes to Donatello.

Once come in favour again, these children, so tremendously alive, spread in the shortest possible time all over the Occident (Note 39). Mantegna (Note 40), Donatello's disciple, made the *putto* familiar throughout upper Italy, both in painting and in sculpture; Lucca della Robbia (Note 41), who worked side by side with Donatello, won over for the *putto* the hearts of the simple and pious people, while Andrea del Verrocchio (Note 42) introduced him to the higher bourgeoisie through his masterpiece, the *putto* with the fish on the fountain in the courtyard of the Palazzo Vecchio in Florence.

The year 1508 is the other decisive year for the *putto* in the West. In that year Raphael started on the frescoes of the Stanze, and Michelangelo on those of the Sistine Chapel in the Vatican. The *putti* assumed in both places new duties to hand down to the following centuries. Most people imagine they know Raphael's Disputa; yet not many will remember the hundreds of *putti* which the master has introduced into the background of the fresco. The scene in heaven is represented like the apse of a church, as a niche. Rays emanate from the upper centre; they look like the meridians on a globe. The cloud-banks on which the saints sit are arranged like the lines of latitude; what Raphael spread out at the back of the scene resembles a picture of the world as well as a picture of the church. The rays are gilded, and between them there are a great number of embossed golden dots. The gold is reminiscent of mediaeval pictures, of the element of eternity they sought to express, and of their detachment from the world. We know that Raphael's era and Raphael himself felt an enthusiastic love for the cosmos. Continents and seas, orbits of planets and suns were discovered; the modern physico-mechanical picture of the world made itself known. Raphael wanted to put the concept of sanctity into this new world, to "represent" it in the original meaning of the word. Therefore he could no longer tolerate a golden background, and so dissolved it into rays and dots. But what appears behind it now? Merely a system of circles, ellipses, parabolas, and hyperboles connected with each other? No; Raphael still professed with Thomas Aquinas that each star has its own angel (Note 43). So he filled his picture of the world with the *putti* of Christian antiquity and of Donatello. He avoided thereby the danger that the newly discovered world might become empty; he comforted the spectator, who might otherwise have feared that the world could be harnessed to the unchangeable determination of mathematics; but, no; the spirits of love support it, playing merrily. And so that no one should be able to call it chance or the whim of a great artist, Raphael re-affirmed by a repetition his belief in the blessed spirits who appear in the shape of children: the background of the Sistine Madonna too (Note 44) is filled with hundreds of *putti*. Rarefied like the atmosphere and yet not to be overlooked, the little spirits from heaven start here on a new task in the history of art. From now on they appear as "decorative angels" wherever an empty space threatens in a picture. The superficial observer might frequently take them for the product of inadequacy. What they really represent, however, is a pictorial profession of faith. No abyss opens in the background where life in the foreground comes to its end; on the contrary, it is just here that the divine wisdom becomes manifest, playing in the shape of an angel-child.

Out of the host of *putti* painted as delicate as gossamer into the fresco of the Disputa, four come to the front (Plate 15). They hold the books of the Gospels to the right and the left of the dove of the Holy Ghost. They are placed exactly on the line where the celestial region finishes and the terrestrial one begins, that is to say on the threshold. The spirit of God Himself steps over this threshold, and the *putti* lead Him, forming with the Word they hold in their hands the step from which He enters the world. According to the mediaeval ruling for pictures in cathedrals, prophets and apostles had to be put on the threshold or at the entrance to the chancel; ".the Word of the Lord is the door." Raphael too still wished to profess this in his painting; but he added that it is the spirits of love who open and shut the door.

It is interesting that the motif of the *putto* on the threshold is repeated in the picture of the Sistine Madonna. Here again two of the numerous angel-children in the background have stolen to the front; they lean over the parapet at the lower edge of the picture (Plate 14). Hardly any angel in the history of art has been reproduced as often as these two. Some spectators have even smiled condescendingly at Raphael's "joke." Yet these angels are of great importance for the composition and meaning of the picture. The threshold at the bottom and the curtain at the top are its fixed and tangible parts, behind which the vision of the Virgin opens up. Everything would fall into a bottomless void without them. Here at the transition from the real to the visionary world lean the *putti*. They are a little like sentries; they could let the curtain fall down and the roguishness of their features even indicates such a possibility. But this they will not do; their eyes guide our gaze upwards. How powerful these eyes are! Everything else about these children is relaxed, even playful, but the eyes turned towards the saint are immobile. What an intense look! The *putti* are mediating between time and eternity.

Michelangelo painted at about the same time the ceiling of the Sistine Chapel (Note 45) not far from Raphael's frescoes. The *putti* were awarded a place in this work too. The idea of the representation was akin to Raphael's. Michelangelo worked, however, with a different method of composition and a different temperament. Forty-eight *putti* are depicted in the lower region of the work behind the prophets and sibyls (Plate 17), where they support the heavens. They stretch and squeeze their small athletic bodies under the timbering, above which unfolds the story of the Bible. So Michelangelo too assigned to the angel-children the zone where heaven and earth touch in the cosmos; they do not, however, perform their task by playing or dancing. Many of them are working hard, some quarrel with each other, others cannot cope with their task. It seems as if too much has been asked of them. They can barely sustain the heavenly vault, and for how much longer? When will it all collapse? Michelangelo perceived this danger threatening his own cosmos, and there is something tragic about his *putti*.

Above the *putti* on the Sistine ceiling are settled twenty *ignudi* (Note 46), the figures of adolescents, some of whom hold garlands with which to decorate the pictures of the Biblical world. These *genii* too belong to the intermediate region, but they are incomparably mightier and more balanced; they are the lords, the *putti* their slaves. They are the *genii* of the world-embracing love as Plato conceived it. Michelangelo painted in his fresco what Dante had described two hundred years before him in the *Vita Nuova*: the genius Amore and his child-like servant the *amoretto*.

Michelangelo too was evidently anxious to confirm his conception by repeating it. The sketches for the tomb of Julius II (Note 47), just like the ceiling of the Sistine Chapel, show a number of genii in the shape of adolescents and a number of *putti*. Here again these figures are placed in the intermediate zone and below the heavenly region; their task is to lead the gaze of the spectator upwards. The designs containing the *putti* have not been carried out, and only four of the *genii* have survived, in a half-finished state. These "slaves" symbolise the encounter of love—in the cosmic meaning of the word as used by Plato—with death. Even if only one of the *putti* had been left us, we would know the reactions of the child-like spirit of love when coming to the threshold of death. A whole century —that of Mannerist art (Note 48), approximately 1520–1620—wrestled with the idea of this representation, but it remained a problem. It made the *putti* ill—as can be seen in the pictures of Bronzino (Note 49) and of Pontormo—there was even some danger that they might disappear from art and depart from life.

However, two great figures of Baroque art, Rubens (Note 50) and Bernini (Note 51) restored them to health and provided them with a new chance of life. Neither of them had anything new to say about the character of the *erotes*; their merit consisted in sorting out, arranging, and spreading out the treasure of ideas and forms gained in the Renaissance. Rubens established something like a scheme for the position, for the task and the meaning of the *putto* in Baroque painting. He evolved permanent types for the *putto* who lifts the curtain, for the *putto* who carries the emblems of the saints, the one who decorates pictures with festoons, sits on cornices, hovers around an aureole of the sacrament or the Holy Spirit. These formulae, tried out by Rubens and his workshop in about three thousand pictures, owed their progress all over the west partly to the fact that Rubens and his engravers introduced them into the illustrations of breviaries and missals. While Rubens's influence was confined mainly to the art of painting, Bernini progressed in sculpture and architecture and assured for the *putto* a place in the whole of Baroque art, on the world-wide stage of the "high-Baroque." The most magnificent example of this will always be the aureole above the altar of the *cathedra* in St Peter's in Rome, a late work of the master, which on a reduced scale is to be found in the "extension" of many Baroque high-altars.

From about a hundred years after Rubens and Bernini date the *putti* to whom above all this small book is dedicated; they are the angel-children of the Swabian-Bavarian baroque churches. They represent the ultimate fruit of a development which had lasted thousands of years. At their time and in their sphere there was no longer any doubt as to the right of existence nor as to the task and the position of these charming creatures. They were now quite at home in the sanctuary. Numerically they held first place among all the other saints and angels who inhabited the church. It is due to them that no one with a sound mind can look at a Bavarian baroque church without a smile.

The main period of their rule started with the end of the seventeenth century, one generation after the end of the Thirty-Years' War. It lasted for three generations until the French Revolution. In the first generation the *putti* organised themselves as it were, in the second they dominated, and in the third they attained their greatest charm, immediately before they met with their irrevocable end. The artists of the first generation (Note 52) were small provincial masters, the grandfathers Schmuzer (Note 53) and Feichtmayr (Note 54) and the last of the Zürns (Note 55) in the Inn district, the old Lorenz Luidl (Note 56) at the Lech. They fulfilled, however, an important task: with the help of the Zuccali (Note 57) and the Viscardi (Note 58) they brought the ideas of the Italian art of the *putti* to the north; yet they retained at the same time their connection with the Rodt (Note 59 and Plate 30) in Illertissen, Reichle in Augsburg (Note 60), Degler at Weilheim (Note 61), Krumpper (Note 62) and the older Zürn of Lake Constance, and through them with Gothic art, from which they repeatedly took over the idea of the child-angel in clothes. True, their *putti* are not as yet very elegant; there they stand somewhat abruptly, carrying the emblems of the saints (a little like figures for the crib in a Nativity scene), and they hang from the beams rather than hover or dance. They still hardly dare to form one of those aureoles above the altar, which later became so popular. However, they make up for this by being, though shy and stiff, quite healthy rustic peasants' children, and while they grew without any break of style right out of the devout Middle Ages, they drew nourishment from the love of the child innate in the Bavarian and the Italian *Modernität* as it was then called.

The second group of *putti*-artists, born towards the end of the seventeenth century, started work at about 1715–1720. Now one hears the great names of the Swabian-Bavarian Baroque, some internationally known for their work in various countries, others deserving world-fame. Johann Michael Fischer (Note 63), Kosmas Damian and Aegid Quirin Asam (Note 64, Plate 32–36), Dominikus Zimmermann (Note 65, Plate 31), Franz Xaver, Johann Michael and Joseph Feuchtmayer, as well as Joseph, the greatest of the brothers Schmuzer. They achieved something unique: out of the German mediaeval heritage and the southern influx originating from antiquity, they created a holy world and supra-world, an unbroken seamless cosmos. This magnificent unity was not without tension and danger. But at the points where the tension was greatest, the masters placed the *putto*, who fastened everything and held it together.

One example of this may be given: These pictures are meant to open up the building to heaven, and by means of an artistic illusion to include heaven within the place of worship. The great problem in this is that of the frame, which might easily trouble the spectator, the transition seeming hard and unconvincing. The court-artists Johann Jakob Zeiller (Note 66, Plate 44), the stucco worker Johann Michael Feichtmayr, and the master-builder Johann Michael Fischer in Otto-beuren solved these problems very ingeniously, in the spandrels of the cupola-frescoes. The painters put the four evangelists into the corners as symbols for the transition from heaven to earth; as mentioned above they had been used for this purpose since the early Christian era. Zeiller painted near the edge of the picture a group of *putti*, supporting the seat and the book of each saint. Feichtmayr, using a sketch by Fischer, set a *stucco-putto* hovering out of the white and gold stucco frame. The *putto's* flesh and his garment are the same colour as those in the fresco, so that picture and architecture are made into one through the means of the same illusion which is effective in the fresco. There are, of course, other devices to unite building and picture. The Asams, for example, liked to let a foot or a hand stick out in relief from the frame. This has sometimes been regarded as artistry rather than art and has tended to prejudice people against the Baroque; in reality the little angel makes us forget art as well as virtuosity, for he is likeable, and while symbolising the bridge he retains his human character.

Another juncture full of tension in Baroque churches is where the altar comes into contact with the architecture of the building. The altars in Baroque churches are built rather like stages. Every theatre-architect knows only too well the difficulties of the transition from the proscenium-arch to the audience. Above and at the sides a curtain, used decoratively, can be of help. The stucco workers of the Baroque age frequently made use of this contrivance. But there was a difficulty: the curtain had to remain open and at the same time be draped in lively folds. The *putti* manage to do this with the utmost ease while playing (Plates 45, 55). Some of the artists had a special liking for this device—more especially Johann Michael Feichtmayr in Zwiefalten and Ottobeuren, Johann Baptist Straub (Note 67) in Berg am Lain, Diessen, Schäftlarn (Plate 60) and Ettal (Plate 24), and Dominikus Zimmermann in Steinhausen, Günzburg, and Wies.

We again feel the tension of the direct physical touch between the visionary and the real world at the base of the altars and pillars of a Baroque church. The first step in the transition is usually accomplished by including the figures of saints. Frequently their flesh and garments are coloured and their whole dress and hair style made to fit Baroque fashion. This is a means of bringing them closer to the spectator. On the other hand these saints show much of the baroque pathos and nearly all of them turn their ecstatic gaze towards heaven, leading away from the spectator and not to him. There again the *putto* proves of help; he nestles against the saint and also attests his attributes. To the spectator these are something like an introduction to the saint. By exhibiting their attributes through the *putti* the saints introduce themselves to us, and establish contact with us. At the same time these attributes in the hands of angel-children are a kind of sermon preached for the spectator, as most of them represent the instruments which were the very reason for the saints passage to heaven (Plates 33, 34, 35, 68, 71, 74).

But the little preachers are anything but gloomy zealots; they bring home their doctrine to the spectator with humour. They are clever. One need only look at the theological programme which the *putti* expound at the altars of Zwiefalten (Johann Michael Feichtmayr, Plate 38) and at the pulpit in Birnau (Joseph Anton Feuchtmayer, Plate 75). Usually the transition by way of an aureole suggested itself to the Baroque architect for the upper zones, where the altar often thrusts forwards, past the height of the architrave, into the region of the frescoes representing heaven. The Holy Trinity is often represented in this extension of the altar, sometimes the figure of the Holy Ghost or of the Lamb or a triangle with the Hebrew name of God, in Jesuit churches the initials of Jesus or Mary in a wreath of rays framed by clouds. Nowhere in the Swabian-Bavarian Baroque is there a wreath of rays like this without some *putti*, whether designed or made by the Asams at Rohr and Aldersbach, Johann Michael Fischer at Osterhofen, Diessen, Zwiefalten, and Ottobeuren, by Dominikus Zimmermann at Günzburg, Steinhausen, Wies, or elsewhere. The presence of a number of *putti* is unavoidable at this point: the situation compels the artist to put them there. Why? The wreath of rays demands a centre from which it emanates; this must be something sun-like; the rays point from there into the whole world. But these rays are not to be thought of as a physical phenomenon; they are a living emanation, they are the powers of love, which emerge from a holy centre. The *erotes* make these powers perceptible (Plate 62). This is also the reason why these child-like spirits are so frequently assembled around the dove of the Holy Ghost (Plate 55) or around the tabernacle of the Most Holy Sacrament (Plates 32, 69)—that is around the spirit of love and the testament of love.

There are two further zones of transition full of tension in Baroque churches: the pulpit and the music-stall, where word and sound become the essential features. The stucco worker or the wood carver added here as a unifying element a dance performed by angel-children and accompanied on the pulpit by the rhythmic voices of the fathers of the church, and on the music-gallery by the gestures of the conductor and the swell of the orchestra. A few specially lovely examples are the *putti*-dance (Plate 54) by Anton Sturm (Note 68) on the pulpit in St. Mang's Church at Füssen, the dancing *putti* embracing each other by Franz Xaver Feichtmayr (Note 69) on the pulpit in Gutenzell (Plate 51), the series of playing and dancing *putti* by Franz Xaver Schmädl in the choir of Rottenbuch (Note 70, Plates 25, 48, 49) and the musician-*putti* by Johann Baptist Straub on the music-stall in the church of the monastery at Diessen.

All these angel-children of Swabia-Bavaria have yet another peculiarity: they are not just children, but are children of the Swabian-Bavarian people, and the painters, stucco workers and wood-carvers were proud fathers showing their own children. This turns the church into a house of children, into the true home of the people. The Swabian-Bavarian Baroque is an art of high rank. This was not accepted until recently, because it is an art that does not fit into museums—and yet there is hardly any art of the same quality in the world as close to the heart of the people as this, mainly because the people find their own children in the church.

About the middle of the eighteenth century, in the lifetime of the third generation of artists, a decisive change took place in the history of human thought. We perceive this clearly when we compare the following two *putti*. The first, of about 1735, stands at Diessen on the Ammersee in the former Augustinian prebendal church; the other, of 1762, hangs in the former Benedictine church at Rott on the Inn (Plate 68). They are suitable for comparison because they are both occupied with the same task. The Diessen-*putto* carries as "attribute-angel" the cardinal's hat of St. Jerome, the Rott-*putto* that of St. Petrus Damianus. Both treat their task as a joke by endeavouring to place the huge hats on their own heads. Xaver Dietrich was originally supposed to have created the group at Diessen, but

32

this has been disputed and there can be no doubt that it was due to Ignaz Günther (Note 71), the architect at the court of the Bavarian Elector, who worked in Rott. The theme given to these two sculptors was the same, but they solved it in a very different manner. St. Jerome in Diessen, in his rustling *cappa magna* and with his solemn gestures, is of a very large size. The prelate by Ignaz Günther is over-slim, turns his body almost as if he were dancing, wears the light habit of a canon and carries a crosier as sole attribute of his dignity—he holds it like a courtier dressed up as a shepherd. His features show definite signs of dissipation, the book in his right hand shows what it is meant to be by its title *Officium Beatae Mariae Virginis*, otherwise one might take it, held as it is by elegantly spread out fingers, for a libertine novel. The cardinal at Diessen stands there as a mighty witness of revelation and faith, the prelate at Rott as representative of the "enlightment." The contrast between these two princes of the church is very clearly reflected in the children accompanying them. The Diessen-*putto* has a magnificent Rubens-like form, he pushes the hat so wildly on to his head that one cannot help smiling; yet this figure is evidently that of a ministrant, serving while firm in his faith. The *putto* above St. Damianus in Rott pays no attention to his master, he is as it were busy trying on his hat in front of a mirror. He is exciting, delightful, but also irreverent—he too is the child of his times. The old faith with its pathos, yet no stranger to humour, speaks to the spectator at Diessen; in Rott the new way of life (philosophy) has found expression with its refined scepticism, leading to irony. Ignaz Günther's *putto* will not remain a ministrant throughout his life; maybe, when grown-up, he will put a Jacobin's cap on his head instead of a cardinal's hat?

The most lovely *putti* of the era of enlightment are in the Cistercian churches at Neu-Birnau and Salem. Joseph Anton Feuchtmayer, Johann Georg Dirr and Johann Georg Wieland (Note 72) made them in stucco, wood, and alabaster.

These masters surprise us first of all by the confidence and freedom with which they represent the most subtle details of children's flesh. Sometimes, however, the sensitive enjoyment of the bodily appearance leads to voluptuousness; the flesh glitters, the gaze of the children is veiled over. The freedom of movement becomes artistic and shows a preference for one stretched out leg. The proportions tend to be over-slim, and remind one of similar forms in the Mannerist period of the late sixteenth century. The angel-children now leave their usual connections; they are no longer essentially figures in frames or spheres of transition. They claim an importance of their own. At the first four side-altars in Birnau, they assume positions which according to older conventions ought to have been reserved for saints (Plate 70). Something similar can be seen on the choir-balustrade at Salem (Plate 77). The *putti* thus leaving their usual connections, lose their unquestioning child-like quality and become thoughtful, sometimes even melancholy. This can be very charming, for instance with the well-known "honey-licking child" in Birnau (Plate 71); it is, however, an indication of the end of an era.

It frightens us still more when the *putti* are made into little angels of death (Plate 80), as was previously done in the sixteenth century. They sink down weeping at the sarcophagi of early Classicism, their limbs have become too heavy for them, they lower the torch of life, meant to resemble an antique torch; it is as if they themselves wanted to lie down and rest. Once more they are roused to a last *scherzo*: they climb up a palm on the organ-gallery of Salem (Plates 78, 79)—do they wish to escape upwards?

The last hour for the Baroque angels came with the French Revolution. The last magnificent church interior of Swabian-Bavarian baroque architecture is the former Benedictine church at Wiblingen near Ulm (Johann Georg Specht, 1772–1778); entering it, we feel an inexplicable sense of emptiness. Columns and beams are grand, but harsh; the altars are now pieces of furniture, which could be placed anywhere. The beautiful frescoes by Januarius Zick, 1732–1797, appear hard above the dazzling white of the walls. Why? No *putti* are left here to unite the different elements. J. Zick's sketch provided for a group of them, for both the pulpit and the baptismal font. But they appear as if hung up and stuck on. Faith in the justification of the *putto* has been lost.

Yet they live on in our thoughts. Goethe evoked them once more in the transfiguration of Faust, and Runge painted them again in his mystical pictures. This is romanticism and as such belongs to the past. Just because they have become things of the past, however, they can teach the spectator the importance of their two thousand years of history; in their forms are revealed a deep intuition and a

sublime faith. Antiquity had a presentiment of it, and Christianity believes that the world—both here and beyond things recognisable, and notwithstanding all apparent contradictions—is held together by the spiritual forces of an all-pervading love. These forces operate while playing, they make the universe one in joy. Plato called this by the untranslatable word *sympatheia ton panton*; The Christian sees this same *sympatheia ton panton* with the vision of his faith; he shares with Plato the conviction that the cosmos is united in love, for he prays to the spirit of wisdom and love, who plays at the knees of the universal Father, and sends out His angels wherever He wishes. The angels are messengers of heavenly love, who appear in the beliefs of pagans, Jews, and Christians; they choose various forms. Sometimes, for example in Pompeii and in the Stanze of the Vatican, as well as in the abbey at Ottobeuren, they present themselves as blessed children.

NOTES

T HE plates of this book tempt us to turn over the pages like those of a picture
    book, which indeed their delightful character would justify. The text has
therefore not been burdened with any references to origin, exact dates etc.
Yet we do not want to leave this book without a scientifically established basis,
and have therefore added to it the following notes, which may contain answers
to some of the questions that are likely to arise.

1. Frits Lugt, Man and Angel, in *Gazette des Beaux Arts*, New York, 1944, I-II.

2. The statements concerning play and religion are based on Hugo Rahner, *Der
   spielende Mensch*, Einsiedeln 1955, 3rd edition. See there also the sources
   of the quotations from the Fathers of the Church.

3. Paulinus of Nola, 353–431, of a Christian senatorial family, and friend of St.
   Ambrosius and St. Martin of Tours; 409 bishop of Nola. 49 letters and 33
   poems of his are extant, and they constitute an important source for the

liturgy of his time and the history of the equipment of churches in early Christianity.

4. Gregory of Nazianzus, 330–390, son of Gregory, bishop of Nazianzus in Asia Minor. Owing to his ten-years' sojourn at the pagan University of Athens, he was better versed in the philosophy and rhetoric of antiquity than any other of the Eastern theologians. Lifelong friend of St. Basil, he joined him in the fight for the doctrine of Trinitarian Orthodoxy. The quotation is taken from the "historical" section of his numerous poetical works; here he treats of the ways of the world in a melancholic vein.

5. Maximus Confessor of Constantinople, 580–662, upheld the doctrine of the Trinity according to the teaching of Gregory of Nazianzus, for whose speeches he wrote a commentary. His Trinitarian Orthodoxy brought him into conflict with the East-Roman Empire and the Eastern Church. He introduced Dionysus the Areopagite into the literature of the church; The Neo-Platonic philosophy of Plotinus as supported by Dionysus underlies this quotation.

6. The Italian word *putto* is derived from the late-Latin word *putus*, meaning little man.

7. The most recent compilation (by Hermine Speyer) of Greek and Roman representations of Eros in sculpture, painting and literature is contained in the *Enciclopedia dell'arte*, Rome 1960. The more recent archaeological literature on the history of the Eros-cult is also to be found there: Adolf Greifenhagen, *Griechische Eroten*, Berlin 1957, and W. Strobel, in a University dissertation at Erlangen in 1952.

8. Hesiod, a Greek poet, eighth century B.C. A Theogony (doctrine of the evolution of the gods) and a Cosmogony (doctrine of the evolution of the world), bear his name; they differ in several respects from Homer's conceptions.

9. It has not been proved that the earliest religious images of Eros had a phallic shape.

10. The image of Aphrodite, the Greek goddess of beauty and love, can be traced back to an Asiatic conception of the fruit-bearing primal mother. (J. R. Harris, *The Origin of the Cult of Aphrodite*, Manchester 1916.) She is married to Hephaistos, the limping god of the blacksmiths; she commits adultery with Ares.

11. Artemis, venerated mainly as goddess of hunting and of wild animals; she was independently of this in more ancient times a goddess of fertility. Her cult began in Asia. The Diana of Ephesus with her hundred breasts, and Eros as god of vegetation (holding a flower in his hand) originate from her. See J. R. Harris, *The Origin of the Cult of Artemis*, Manchester 1916.

12. Ares, the god of war, of much later date than Aphrodite, was first introduced into Greek mythology by Homer. The connection between Aphrodite and Ares probably has a ritual basis (their places of veneration were near to each other), as well as an allegorical meaning; harmony is produced when male ferocity and female beauty unite. See O. Kern, *Die Religion der Griechen*, Berlin 1926, I. p. 119, and U.v. Willamowitz-Moellendorff, *Der Glaube der Hellenen*, Berlin 1931, I. p. 323.

13. Hermes, the resourceful god of wanderers, shepherds, servants and thieves, was originally a purely Hellenic god, with no fixed abode or place of veneration; he hovers about between Olympos, Earth and Hades, and also leads the souls to the latter. This is probably the origin of the all-uniting character

of Eros. See K. Kerényi, *Hermes der Seelenführer*, Zürich, 1944. Kerényi calls Eros "a somewhat idealised and slightly more stupid son of Hermes."

14. Praxiteles, a Greek sculptor, 392-330 B.C., first representative of a late-classical, softer and psychologically more expressive style.

15. Euripides, Greek tragedian, 484-406 B.C.; in contrast to the orthodox Sophocles, he adhered to the Sophists' enlightment and introduced Eros with bow and arrow into his tragedy *Medea*.

16. The lofty Eros is the Eros Uranios, the lower one the Eros Pandemos; he derived these names from his mother Aphrodite, who had been venerated as a goddess of celestial love, Aphrodite Urania, and as goddess of the love of simple people, Aphrodite Pandemos.

17. The Orphics were a religious sect of the sixth century B.C. which originated in Thrace. They had a theogony and a cosmogony of their own, independent of the Greek one; they spread chiefly to Southern Italy. The Orphic Mysteries promised to save their adherents from the underworld. In their later forms they show certain affinities with Christianity. See W. Willi, "Die orphischen Mysterien und der griechische Geist," in *Eranos-Jahrbuch*, 11, 1944.

18. Plato, Greek philosopher, 427-347 B.C., disciple of Socrates, established in his dialogue *Symposion* the idea of the Eros in philosophy; Eros is the son of Poros (way, means) and of Peneia (poverty), and evokes in the soul the memory of the primal forms of the ideas. See K. Kerényi, *Der grosse Daemon des Symposion*, Amsterdam 1942.

19. The Hellenistic phase began in the Empire of Alexander the Great (founded about 330 B.C.); its centre was in Alexandria. It proved to be a mixed and fruitful Graeco-Oriental civilisation and spread all over the Mediterranean, dominating intellectual life until the time of Augustus (31 B.C.).

20. Pan was the Greek god of the woods and fields, son of Hermes and a nymph; his whole body was covered with hair and he had the horns and feet of a goat. At first he was the prolific multiplier of herds, later, under the influence of Eros, his main occupation was the pursuit of nymphs and shepherd-boys. In addition to this "singular" god Pan, many small Pans are mentioned by Aristophanes, who are called Paniskes, similar to the Erotes beside Eros. In the theological philosophy of the late Middle Ages and the Baroque Pan is often interpreted as the devil. His image therefore influenced that of the devil as it was conceived in these epochs. Profane pictures of the Baroque also often show Paniskes, especially at the feasts of Dionysus. See Reinhard Herbig, "Der Gestaltwandel Pans in der griechischen Kunst," in *Pan, der griechische Bocksgott*, Versuch einer Monographie," Frankfurt am Main, 1949.

21. Apuleius, Roman poet from Madaura in Numidia, 125–180 A.D., author of an adventure-novel, called "Metamorphoses," modelled on Greek stories. The fairy-tale of "Amor and Psyche" forms a chapter of it. As philosopher Apuleius belongs to the intermediate Platonists preparing the way for Neo-Platonism. See A. Dyroff, *Das Märchen von Amor und Psyche*, Cologne 1941.

22. Ovid (Publius Ovidius Naso), Roman poet 43 B.C.–18 A.D., wrote "Amores" (love elegies), "Heroides" (love letters of heroines), "Ars Amandi" (the art of loving), "Remedia Amoris" (remedies against love), "De Medicamine Faciei" (cosmetics) and "Metamorphoses" (changes of form).

23. Lucian, Greek satirical author, contemporary of Apuleius, 120–180 A.D., best known through his "Conversations of Hetaerae." At first he was a follower of the so-called Second Sophism, but was soon disgusted by the

insincerity and the mere verbosity of the late Hellenism, and became the greatest satirist of late Antiquity.

24. Virgil (Publius Vergilius Maro), Roman poet, 70–19 B.C., wrote "Bucolica" (shepherds' songs), "Georgica" (songs on country life) and the Roman national epic "The Aeneid."

25. Alkman, Greek poet, about 645 B.C., head of the Doric school of poets in Sparta, and choirmaster of virgin's choirs. "Virgin song of Artemis."

26. For the history of the early Christian era see mainly *Dictionnaire d'archéologie chrétienne et de liturgie*, edited by F. Cabrol and H. Leclercq, Paris 1924 ff. and *Reallexikon für Antike und Christentum* edited by Th. Klauser, Stuttgart 1941.

27. We find *erotes* harvesting grapes on the sarcophagus and the mosaics of Santa Costanza in Rome, on the sarcophagus in the Lateran which shows the Good Shepherd three times, on paintings in the Domitilla catacomb and on the Junius Bassus sarcophagus in the Vatican (Junius Bassus was prefect of Rome, born 317; he was baptised and died 359).

28. See the article "Eros" by Hermine Speyer in *Enciclopedia dell' arte*, Rome 1960.

29. See Joh. Jak. Bachofen, "Urreligion und Symbole," *Gesammelte Werke* 1951.

30. M. Collington quotes from *Dictionnaire d'archéologie chrétienne et de liturgie*.

31. St. Nilus (senior) died after 426. He was prefect of Constantinople, later Superior of a congregation of monks at Ankyra in Asia Minor; he wrote as an ascetic author to his younger friend Olympiodorus (died after 450), who was a pagan historian at the Imperial Court of Byzantium. (Quoted from Ch. Diehl, *Manuel d'art byzantin*, Paris 1925–26). See Joseph Wilpert, *Die römischen Mosaiken und Malereie*, p. 3ff.

32. For the mediaeval conceptions of *amor* and *caritas* and for the change occurring at Dante's time (1265–1321) see Edouard Wechsler, "Eros und Minne", in *Vorträge der Bibliothek Warburg* 1921, p. 69ff. and Franz Wickhoff, "Die Gestalt Amors in der Phantasie des italienischen Mittelalters" in *Jahrbuch der kgl. preussischen Kunstsammlungen*, 1890/XI. The quotations from Dante are taken from the last-mentioned essay.

33. For the thousand years of angels, see Ernest Buschor, "Das Zeitalter der Engel," in *Festschrift* for Professor Jantzen 1931.

34. Giovanni Boccaccio, 1313–1375, humanist and reviver of Greek studies; author of *Decamerone*, which he himself condemned after his conversion in 1361. He was the first man to lecture on Dante. His inseparable friend was Francesco Petrarch.

35. Petrarch (Francesco Petrarca), 1304–1374, Poeta Laureatus in Rome 1341; most famous through his *Canzoniere* dedicated to his love for Laura.

36. Piero Tedesco and Niccolo d'Arezzo (as well as Antonio di Banco) made as yet undeveloped *putti* for the southern and northern doors respectively of the cathedral at Florence.

37. Donatello (Donato di Niccolo di Betto Bardi), 1386–1466, was the greatest artist of the early Renaissance in Italy; it is considered his particular merit to have imbued the classical ideal of art with Christian meaning. See H. Kaufmann, *Donatello*, Berlin 1936.

38. Walter F. Otto, *Menschengestalt und Tanz*, Munich 1958.

39. The progress of the *putto* all over Europe found one limit only: the world of the icon; the *putto* always remained alien to it.

40. Andrea Mantegna, 1431–1506, the most important Venetian painter of the early Renaissance, made the achievements of the Florentine artists known in Northern Italy. See F. Knapp, *Mantegna*, Berlin 1924.

41. The della Robbia were a Florentine family of artists: Luca, 1399–1482, his nephew Andrea, 1435–1525, and Giovanni, the most efficient of his sons, 1469–1529. They popularised the art of the early Italian Renaissance; their greatest success in achieving this sprang from their use of glazed clay.

42. Andrea del Verrocchio, 1436–1488, Donatello's successor in art as well as in the service of the Medici, worked chiefly in bronze. His main feat with regard to the *amoretto* was the dolphin-*putto* for the Villi Careggi, now in the Palazzo Vecchio at Florence. For the development of the *putto* in the early years of Italian Renaissance see also W. Bode, "Versuche der Ausbildung des Genre in der florentinischen Plastik des Quattrocento," in *Jahrbuch der kgl. preussischen Kunstsammlungen*, 1890/XI.

43. On Aquinas's faith in stars and angels see Martin Grabmann, *Das Seelenleben des hl. Thomas von Aquin*, Munich 1924. It is unlikely that either Raphael or Michelangelo knew Aquinas; but both were well versed in the writings of Dante, in whose *Convivio* angels, archangels and thrones move the planets. See Anton Springer, *Raphael und Michelangelo*, Leipzig 1896, II, p. 376.

44. Raphael painted the Sistine Madonna in about 1516 for the Monastery of San Sisto in Piacenza. St. Barbara and St. Sisto, the pope who gave his name to the picture, kneel beside the Virgin. The monastery sold the picture to Dresden in 1754 where it remained until the end of the war in 1945; after an exile in Russia it returned there.

45. The Sistine Chapel in the Vatican, built in 1473–1481, and named after its founder Pope Sisto IV, is the private chapel of the Popes. The upper part

of its side-walls are covered with frescoes of the *quattrocento*. Commissioned by Julius II, Michelangelo started painting the vault in 1508; he finished it in 1512.

46. For Michelangelo's attitude with regard to Platonism, which can be deduced from the figures of the *ignudi* and the *erotes* on the Sistine vault, see Carl Tomay, *Michelangelo II, The Sistine Ceiling*; by the same author, "La volta della Capella Sixtina", in *Bolletino d'arte*, No. IX, 1936, and by the same author "Werk und Weltbild des Michelangelo," in *Albae Vigiliae*, Zürich, 1949.

47. The tomb commissioned by Julius II for himself in 1505 was planned in so gigantic dimensions that it turned out to be the tragedy of Michelangelo's life as an artist. Such of it as has been preserved is dispersed, the "slaves" in Florence and Paris and the magnificent Moses, put up unknown to Michelangelo in San Pietro in Vincoli in Rome. For the latter's composition see the drawing by Jacopo Sacchetti, reproduced in Hans Makkowsky, *Michelangelo*, Stuttgart 1941, p. 134.

48. The preference of Mannerist Art for the *putto* holding a skull in his hand has been treated by Horst W. Janson in "The Putto with the Death's head," in *The Art Bulletin*, 1937, p. 423. In Classicism patrons and artists came back to the death-*erotes*.

49. Agnolo Bronzino, 1503–1563, disciple of Michelangelo in Florence, and Jacopo da Pontormo, 1494–1557, elongated the child-bodies of the *putti* in a morbid manner and imbued their features with a terrifying sadness anything but child-like; this too is repeated towards the end of the Baroque, for example in the *putti* of the churches at Birnau and Salem.

50. Peter Paul Rubens,1577–1640, a Flemish artist, pupil of the Jesuits from 1600–1608 in Italy and Spain, therefore thoroughly conversant with both the

classical and the Christian tradition, combined his sound strength with the verve of the counter-reformation and the open mind of the courtier, and formed of this a work of art as forcible as that of Michelangelo, as colourful as that of Titian, and as huge as no other in history. See Hans-Gerhard Evers, *Peter Paul Rubens*, Munich 1942, and by the same author *Rubens und sein Werk*, Brussels 1944 (this volume contains the etchings from breviary and missal).

51. Giovanni Lorenzo Bernini, 1598-1680, Neapolitan by birth, Roman by choice and profession, architect, sculptor and painter, artistic adviser and "general inspector" to six popes, gave Rome its Baroque look. His was a life of glowing passions and at the same time of profound piety. See R. Wittkower, *Giovanni Lorenzo Bernini*, London 1955.

52. Most of the *putti* reproduced here are in the churches described by Norbert Lieb in his book *Barockkirchen zwischen Donau und Alpen*, Munich 1958. There he gives exact dates and lists of the works of art important for the history of style of south German Baroque, dividing it according to the artists' generations; he also shows the family relations of the artists and the connections between the patrons and the artists. For an addition to this see Michael Hartig, *Die oberbayerischen Stifte*, 2 vols, Munich 1935, and by the same author *Die niederbayerischen Stifte*, Munich 1939.

53. The Schmuzers from Wessobrunn worked for five generations as builders and stucco workers in the Swabian-Bavarian Baroque: Jörg and Matthias I worked at the beginning of the seventeenth century; their sons are Matthias II, 1634-1686, and Johann, 1642-1701. Then there came Johann's son Franz I, 1676-1741, and his brother Joseph, born 1683; the latter's son Franz II,

1713–1775, was the last artist of this old family; see Norbert Lieb, *Ottobeuren und die Barockarchitektur*, Munich 1933.

54. Feichtmayr (Feuchtmayer). Of the numerous lines of this family two branches are to be distinguished from among the others: one of them comes from Wessobrunn; to this belong Kaspar, born 1639, Magnus Feichtmayr, born 1679, Franz Xaver Feichtmayr, 1705–1764, and his brother Johann Michael, 1709–1772. The other branch was domiciled in Linz and then moved to the district of Lake Constance; its members were: Franz Joseph, 1659–1718, and Joseph Anton, 1696–1770, the artist of the "honey licker" in Birnau, and Johann Michael Feichtmayr, the highly gifted stucco worker of Ottobeuren.

55. Jörg Zürn, 1581–1635, is the artist of the high altar at Ueberlingen, the master-piece of early Baroque in Germany. His brothers Martin and Michael, working between 1624 and 1665, took his art with them to the Inn-district of Upper-Austria.

56. Lorenz Luidl (Loidl, Loydl), died 1719, was the master of the altars in the church dedicated to the ascension of the Virgin in Landsberg. He was the father of Johannes Sebastian and of Stephan Luidl, who had their workshops at Landsberg and at Dillingen, and even manufactured *putti* for sale.

57. The Zuccali came from the Grisons: Kaspar, 1629–1678, Johann Kaspar, who died 1717, court-architect in Salzburg, and the most important of them, Enrico, 1642–1724, chief architect at the court of Munich. He built the Theatins' church, designed the facade of St. Mary's Minster in Ettal, and thereby gave a decisive stimulus to the whole of the Bavarian Baroque.

58. Giovanni Antonio Viscardi, 1647–1713, also from the Grisons, was Bavarian court architect before and after Enrico Zuccali; he surpassed the latter in that he succeeded in transforming the Italian Baroque into a German one. His most important works are the Trinity Church in Munich, Neustift near Freising, and the former Cistercian church at Fürstenfeldbruck.

59. Christoph Rodt, 1475/80–1634, author of the high-altar of Illertissen.

60. Hans Reichle, 1570–1636, author of the more than life-sized bronze group of St. Michael at the Arsenal in Augsburg; there are two pairs of war-like " hero-*putti*" there.

61. Hans Degler of Weilheim, died 1637, author of the three large altars of St. Ulrich in Augsburg.

62. Hans Krumpper of Weilheim, 1570–1634, sculptor at the court of the Elector Maximilian I of Bavaria; he was a disciple of Hubert Gerhaert. His works were the first in the style of early Bavarian Baroque in Munich; he made the Patrona Bavariae for the Residence in Munich. The "hero-*putti*" at the Virgin's Column in Munich were made by an artist from his circle.

63. Johann Michael Fischer, 1691–1766, built thirty-two churches and twenty-three monasteries and convents; among them those in Diessen, Zwiefalten, Ottobeuren and Berg am Laim.

64. The Asam family: the father, Hans Georg, 1649–1711, was a painter. His sons were Kosmas Damian, 1686–1739, and Aegid Quirin, 1692–1750. Both spent two years, 1712–1714, studying in Rome. Kosmas Damian was a

painter and architect, Aegid Quirin a sculptor and architect. Among their principal works are Weltenburg, Rohr, St. Nepomuk in Munich and the former Premonstratensian church in Altenmarkt near Osterhofen.

65. Dominikus Zimmermann, 1685–1766, stuccoer in Wessobrunn, builder of altars and master-builder; his main buildings are: Steinhausen, Günzburg, Wieskirche. His brother Johann Baptist Zimmermann, 1680–1758, stuccoer and Bavarian court-painter, was at his best when he worked together with his brother at Steinhausen and Wies.

66. Johann Jakob Zeiller, 1710–1783, was a painter; he studied in Rome and Vienna; his are the large frescoes in Ettal, Ottobeuren and Oberammergau. He had a special gift of adjusting his groups to the space of the church interior and so in creating a unity of the architecture, stucco-work and painting; hardly any other painter succeeded in this as well as he did.

67. Johann Baptist Straub, 1704–1784, sculptor at the Bavarian court, disciple of Raphael Donner in Vienna; the altars and pulpits in Fürstenfeld, Berg am Laim, Schäftlarn and Ettal bear witness to his talent. His asymmetrical compositions with figures in a dreamlike, almost tired mood, fit into the buildings in a manner similar to the paintings of Zeiller and just as well.

68. Anton Sturm, 1690/95–1757, sculptor from Füssen, made the figures of the four Fathers of the church in the nave of the church at Wies, and the dance of the *putti* below the pulpit at St. Mang's Church in Füssen.

69. Franz Xaver Feichtmayr, 1705–1764.

70. Franz Xaver Schmädl, 1705–1777, sculptor from Weilheim, made in about 1735 the *putti* in Diessen, those in Andechs in about 1755 and the musician-*putti* of Rottenbuch in about 1744.

71. Ignaz Günther, 1725-1775, a sculptor, worked mostly in wood; he made almost all the decorations in Rott on the Inn. Other important works of his are in Weyarn, Neustift near Freising, Starnberg and Attel.

72. Johann Georg Dirr, 1723–1779, a sculptor, decorated the church of the former Cistercian abbey at Salem, assisted by his son-in-law Johann Georg Wieland.

DESCRIPTIONS OF DRAWINGS
AND PLATES

Some of the drawings interspersed among the text are reproductions of the drawings made by Dürer for the Emperor Maximilian's Book of Hours. Hans Schönberger in Augsburg was commissioned in 1512 to print a Book of Hours for the Emperor. This was printed in 1513 and illustrated from 1515 onwards by various artists, but it was never completed. Albrecht Dürer (1471–1528) made marginal drawings for about fifty of the parchment leaves of the book. The original is in the State Library at Munich (see pages 7, 9, 12, 20, 35, and 74).

The *putto* on stilts on p. 29 forms part of Dürer's engraving "The Doctor's Dream," 1497–1499.

Six silverpoint drawings by Ignaz Günther, 1725–1775, are to be found on pages 1, 5, 17, 37, 50, and 51.

The following numbers refer to the plates at the end of the book.

* * *

1. Eros with flower in front of an altar. Cup found at Vulci, 460 B.C.; diameter of inside-picture 14 cm.; Museum of Antiquities in Munich. The picture of Eros is still classical in style; the winged youth holds the symbol of life and love in his hands.

2. *Erotes* playing with hoops on a sarcpohagus of the fourth century B.C. Museo Chiaramonti in the Vatican Collections. The hoops are spherical. These childish games of the *erotes* symbolise the play of the gods with the globe of the world.

3. *Erotes* racing with chariots; Roman marble relief. Representation of *putti* occupied in the games or sports of adults were popular in antiquity. See also plates 26 and 27.

4. Sarcophagus of the second century A.D., showing four *genii* as door-keepers at the line where the realms of life and death meet. It is no longer possible to see any difference between *genii* and *erotes*; all these figures are comforters, promising love and life. Sala dei Trionfi, Palazzo dei Conservatori, Rome.

5. Eros and Psyche in a flower garden, third century A.D., after the fairy-tale by Apuleius (p. 41, Note 21). Gallery of the Flavii in the catacomb of Domitilla, Rome.

6. Funeral urn of Lucilius Felix with pine-cone as symbol of everlasting life. Period of Hadrian, Capitolinian Museum, Rome. The octagonal base of the urn suggested to the sculptor a figure-of-eight circle for his dancing and playing musician-*putti*. The theme, shown here in small size, is taken up 1400 years later on a larger scale by Donatello in his *erotes'* dances on the pulpits and singers' galleries at Florence and Prato.

7. *Putto* with dolphin, small bronze 60 cm. high, from Pompeii, National Museum at Naples; about A.D. 50 (No. 111701). In Hellenistic and Roman times the figure of the *amorino* with the dolphin was more frequent than any other *putto* figure. According both to ancient and modern science, and to myths and fairy tales, the dolphin is one of the most friendly of animals; since the time of Homer it has been associated with nearly every god and hero (Odysseus' shield shows a dolphin) and in particular with Aphrodite and Eros, for it gives and arouses affection everywhere.

8. *Putto* with staff and fillet from the vault of the Flavii in the catacomb of Domitilla, Rome; approximately A.D. 200. The original of this motif can be traced back to pre-Christian times. He displays the insignia of the worship of the dead, as assistant to the priest like the ministrants and child-angels of later years.

9. *Erotes* harvesting grapes; sarcophagus, end of third century; Lateran Museum, Rome. See text p. 14.

10/11. At Aquileia, a harbour town of late antiquity, a room for public worship was founded by Bishop Theodor, 308–319. One of the large panels of the mosaic floor shows the story of the prophet Jonah. Several fisher *putti-erotes*, most of them with wings, make it a very lively picture. An inscription states that Bishop Theodor had recently died; therefore the mosaic must have been made about

320. Stylistically these *putti* occupy an important place between early Christian and Byzantine mosaics (G. Brusin-P. L. Zovato, *Monumenti paleocristiani di Aquileia e di Grado*, Udine 1957).

12. *Putti* playing. One of the numerous bas-reliefs which Agostino d'Antonio di Duccio, born 1418, died before 1498, made for the Tempio Malatestiano at Rimini between the years 1447 and 1454.

13. Bronze-*putto* by Donatello, from the font of the Baptismal Chapel at Siena. See text p. 21.

14. Detail of Sistine Madonna, 1516, in the Grüne Gewölbe at Dresden. Rafaello Santi, 1483–1520. See text p. 23.

15. Detail of the Disputa, 1512, by Rafaello Santi, 1483–1520, in the Vatican. See Note 44.

16. The *putti* on the choir-stalls of Santa Giustina in Padua, *circa* 1560, are the work of a provincial master. They are of particular interest, because two sources of tradition merge here. Mediaeval pictures often showed angels performing the services of deacons; in the fourteenth and fifteenth centuries it became more and more usual to depict these tasks as entrusted to child-angels. These child-angels are not *putti*. If we look at Stefan Lochner's pictures of the Virgin, we see that these figures, wearing surplices, albes, and stoles, and holding candles, censers, and missals, are winged ministrants. In Santa Giustina these ministrants are represented as *putti*; they are shown naked in classical postures. Two different streams of the play-element in religious art are combined here.

17. This is one of the pairs of *putti* of which Michelangelo painted one over each of the prophets and sibyls on the vault of the Sistine Chapel, 1508–1512. Life's joy and agony, the delight and the worries of creative work, love-play and

love-tiff are shown together in these groups. The group reproduced here is above the picture of the prophet Daniel.

18. Three *genii* with helmet and shield, an engraving by Albrecht Dürer, 1500–1505 (Bartsch 66). After the Renaissance the *putti* act more and more often as bearers of heraldic devices. They admit thereby their descent from the *genii* on antique sarcophagi, where they held the *clipeus*. They guarantee love and life to the owner of the coat of arms.

19. The four hero-*putti* on the base of the Virgin's Column in Munich symbolise the fight against plague, war, hunger, and heresy. They were cast in about 1638 by the Munich bell-founder Bernhard Ernst. The artist who made the models is still uncertain; of late they have been ascribed to Georg Petel, 1590–1633, born at Weilheim, Upper Bavaria. The column was dedicated by the Elector Maximilian I. to the Padrona Bavariae in thanksgiving for the deliverance of the two capitals, Munich and Landshut, in the Thirty Years' War. Planned 1630, finished 1638.

20/21. Raymond de la Fage, 1656–1690, gave here an iconographic summary of the most popular *putto*-motifs: harvest, bread, wine, music. In doing so he went back—probably unconsciously—to the conceptions of antiquity.

22. *Putto* in the choir-stall of the Fuggers' Chapel in St. Anna in Augsburg, originally the church of the Carmelite monastery. The west-choir was donated in 1509 by Jakob and Ulrich Fugger, and decorated by Hans Daucher and Sebastian Loscher, working together 1510–1518. The *putto* by Sebastian Loscher is in a meditative mood; he holds a ball as the *erotes* on the sarcophagus of the fourth century in the Vatican played with hoops and balls. In both instances there is the *sphaira*, the celestial circle, and in both the *erotes* are cosmic *erotes*.

23. Palm carrying *putto* beside the Johannes Nepomuk statue opposite the pulpit in Rottenbuch, carved in wood, painted white and polished by Franz Xaver Schmädl (1744). The country craftsman's grasp of form reaches right to the highly intellectual mysticism of the late Baroque.

24. Hovering *putto* at the altar of the Holy Family in the minster at Ettal, carved in wood, painted white and polished, by Johann Baptist Straub, 1745. The child moves with courtly elegance to the tune of a minuet. Slight tiredness and melancholy are spread over its dreaming little face.

25. *Putto* with lute, painted white and polished; organ-gallery in Rottenbuch (companion statue to Pl. 49) made by Franz Xaver Schmädl in 1744. The child, confidently playing, symbolises the rough gay peasants' music, which still resounds every Sunday from this same organ-gallery.

26/27. *Putti* chariot-racing with dolphins, and *putti* trafficking in oil. In the reception room in the house of the Vetti at Pompeii, first century B.C. It is in the encaustic technique; i.e. hot wax superimposed on a thick layer of stucco; half original size. These little pictures are part of a long row, which forms a frieze all round the room at a sitting spectator's eye-level. The charming little figures are designed with the particular intention of making them achieve the impossible: while playing, they do the work of adults, often in an impossible but amusing way, like a chariot-race in water.

28/29. *Putti* defend the fig harvest against a pilfering long-tailed monkey, but are frightened by an attacking stag-beetle. So-called "Posch-missal," 1526; Library of the Augustinian prebendary monastery at Neustift near Brixen. Miniature painting in *tempera*, relieved with gold. Late Gothic and Renaissance miniature painting once again took up the predilection of late Antiquity for the so-called grotesques. Sacred texts are framed with witty marginal figures, which generally have no connection with the contents of the page, but instil into the sacred earnestness of the liturgy a joyful though pious love of the world. This applies also to Dürer's Book of Hours for Maximilian.

30. Musician-angel accompanied by a *putto* with a flute and by two singing *putti*. On the high-altar in St. Martin's parish church at Illertissen. It was carved in wood and painted on about 1604 by Christoph Rodt of Neuburg-Kammel, 1575/80-1634. The shrine of the altar, still conceived in a crypto-Gothic style, represents the Virgin's assumption and her coronation in heaven. The holy scene is surrounded by a wreath of musician-angels and *putti*. The angel-children are copied from Italian and Flemish bronze *putti*. It is interesting to see how naturally they perform their gay tasks, side by side with the serious "adult" angels.

31. *Putto* lying on an archivolt. In the church of the former Carthusian monastery at Buxheim. Made not before 1709 by Dominikus Zimmermann (1685–1766). Both the archivolt and the *putto* are in stucco-marble; the *putto* is coloured and partly gilded, and the shape of his body shows a surprising similarity with Rubens's figures. The importance of this *putto* lies in the ease with which its colour and movements break the space and lead over from the heaviness of the archivolt to the white stucco wall.

32/33. Two groups of *putti*, one with a monstrance, the other with confession-stole, book, and tongue-reliquary. In the church of the former Premonstratensian Abbey Osterhofen-Altenmarkt. It was built in 1728 by Johann Michael Fischer and decorated with frescoes by Kosmas Damian Asam; by 1735 sculptures by Aegid Quirin Asam (1692–1750) had been added. The two groups adjoin at the large altars of the central chapels. To the north St. Norbert, the founder of the order, kneels in the light of the window before the hovering monstrance. To the south St. Johannes Nepomuk kneels before the Virgin, who offers him the laurel wreath of victory; at his side are angel-boys, with stole, penitential belt, book, and tongue-reliquary. These groups are made in a technique which employs both wood and stucco; they are somewhat larger than life-size, coloured, and partly relieved with gold. The group around the monstrance belongs to the class known as aureole-angels. The little angels, consisting only of heads and wings, are not really *putti*; they are cherubim figures, made to resemble *putti*; their original place, according to their theological character, was only near the throne of God; but gradually less attention was paid to this, and they came to be used anywhere practically as decoration. The aureole-*putti* are always arranged like radii around a centre and are always connected with rays. They indicate that the rays not only imitate physical phenomena of light, but are living emanations of divinity.

The *putti* of the other group are so-called attribute-angels. Here they produce the "instruments" through which St. Johannes Nepomuk went to heaven. Patron of confessional secrecy, distinguished by his spiritual learning, he was a keen and conscientious confessor, and preferred martyrdom to the violation of the confessional secret. His tongue remained uninjured after his death. The *putto* on the right directs our attention to this by lifting the tongue-reliquary. The inscription *secretum meum mihi* (I keep my secret) is a quotation from the Bible, and points to the eloquence of sermons in the Baroque era. The attribute-angels are often pictorial sermon illustrations, or themes for sermons.

34/35. *Putti* with banderols. For place and master see Plates 32/33. These *putti* stand on the plainer side-altars on the northern side, and are dedicated to St. Dionysius, John the Baptist, and St. John the Evangelist. The legend says that after he had been beheaded St. Dionysius carried his head to the place of burial: " S. Dionysium proditur abscissum suum caput sustulisse." And the Lord's word "si mortiferum quid biberint . . ." "if they drink something deadly, it will not harm them" is believed to have come true in the case of St. John the Evangelist, when the poison beaker given to him broke to pieces and a serpent came out of it. The angels with the banderols, even more than the attribute-angels, are meant to be looked upon as little preachers, who intone the *panegyricus* for their saints.

The two shown here are of an unusually delicate and almost classically restrained build; their contraposition is less accentuated than is usual in Bavaria. This style, which lasted for a short phase between the German high-Baroque and the Rococo, is sometimes called Regence; it is distinguished by courtly elegance, and prefers the erudite banderols to the more simple attribute.

36. *Putto* holding the fringe of the bishop's mantle. For place, date and master see Plates 32–35. This *putto* on the St. Norbert altar holds the train of the praying saint. This is a kind of attribute-angel in close contact with the main figure. Bishops were accompanied by a *caudatarius* (trainbearer); the angel-boy has taken over this function with light-hearted playfulness. He relieves the ceremonious duty of its frequently oppressive seriousness.

37. Weeping *putto*. In the church of the former Augustinian prebendal Abbey at Weyarn, built in the high-Baroque era and decorated with wood sculptures by Ignaz Günther (1725–75), among them an Annunciation and a Lamentation of the Virgin. These groups, made in 1764, can be carried in procession. The *putto* reproduced here is busy with the shroud of the *pietà* group in the same man-ner as the *putto* in the previous picture was busy with the bishop's mantle, but he has no duty to fulfil; he shares most sincerely in the sorrow of the main figures, but there is some comfort to be felt in his own sorrow. Ignaz Günther could not bear to confront the spectator with unrelieved severity of pathetic suffering, and

had to find some way out to a lesser affliction: this is the *putto* who makes us smile among tears.

38. *Putto* dancing with a lamb, 1750. In the church of the former Benedictine Abbey at Zwiefalten, finished by Johann Michael Fischer in about 1745, and decorated with stucco by Johann Michael Feichtmayr (1709–1772) by 1765. At the first side-altar in the transept to the right, dedicated to John the Baptist, the coloured stucco-*putto* dances with the gilded stucco lamb which accompanies the saint as his attribute. The *putto* points with his left hand to the saint, but with his left one only, for his main task, which he shares with numerous other *putti*, is to create the impression of hovering and dancing in the church.

39. Soldier-*putti*. For place see Plate 38. The group of Ezekiel is placed as a counterpart opposite the large pulpit of the abbey church. The big central figure of the preaching prophet was made by Joseph Christian of Riedlingen, the decoration and the figures at the edges, God the Father and twelve *putti*, by Johann Michael Feichtmayr (1709–1772) in about 1750. The reproduction here shows a detail referring to the Babylonian captivity of the prophet. The warlike *putto* to the left symbolizes Sedekias, King of Judah; that to the right, with the lion's skin over his head, symbolises Nebukadnezzor, King of Babylon, holding the plan of that town in his hand. It is evident that the erudite scheme of an abbey theologian has been carried out here, and it is thanks to the children who master it playfully that the dry doctrine has not become boring.

40. *Putto* with bow and arrow and a bandage over his eyes. For place and date see Plate 38. The figure is at the fourth side-altar to the right; it is made of stucco and toned to look like alabaster. The altar is dedicated to St. Agnes, whose death is represented in the central picture. Beside it is the symbolic figure of celestial love, warding off terrestrial love—the *putto* with bow and arrow. It is a sad example

of the rent in the conception of love, due to the misunderstood doctrines of the counter-reformation, found often in ascetic literature. The *putto* has lost his wings and his eyes have been blindfolded—this had never been done in Antiquity, in spite of all the complaints about the blindness of love.

41. *Putto* in a *rocaille* cartouche, holding bunches of flowers, 1749. For place see Plate 38. This shell-work cartouche of *stucco bianco* with gold decoration belongs to the vault of the side-aisle to the right, below a fresco by Mainrad von Aw, which represents a scene from the life of the Virgin. The cartouche connects the vault with the architrave above the side-wall. On the gold background, enlivened by ornaments, the blessed children can be seen romping about above a bank of clouds. They tell the spectator that there is no place without life in the heaven of a Baroque church.

42. *Putto* holding a thunderbolt in his right hand, 1767. This and the following five pictures are taken from the church of the Benedictine abbey at Ottobeuren. Erected by Johann Michael Fischer, with paintings by Johann Jakob Zeiller and with sculptures by Joseph Christian and by Johann Michael Feichtmayr (1709–1772), it became the most important Swabian-Bavarian Baroque building, 1748–1766. Following Benedictine tradition it was primarily dedicated to the veneration of the holy angels. Under its roof there are many hundreds of figures of angels, including *putti*. Johann Michael Feichtmayr found here a natural and matter-of-fact form of movement for his angel-children. The *putto* with the thunderbolt in his right hand stands beside the St. Michael of Joseph Christian on the first side-altar to the left. The thunderbolt indicates that St. Michael is a patron saint, who protects against the plague. The *putto* is not throwing forth the thunderbolt, which the avenging God has launched, but catches it by order of the archangel before it reaches its destination.

43. *Putto* gathering a curtain. For place, date, and master see Plate 42. Diagonally opposite St. Michael's altar at the juncture of the nave and the cupola is situated St. Joseph's altar. The chief figure, by Johann Christian, is of white stucco; the *putti* in the decoration by Johann Michael Feichtmayr have natural flesh tints. The *putto* grasps the drapery which frames the altar like a stage-curtain. He emerges from shadowy depths and thus repeats the theme of the main figure: humility smiling cheerfully from the background.

44. *Putto* between picture and frame. For place see Plate 42. The fresco of St. Matthew the Evangelist, 1763, by Johann Jakob Zeiller (1710–1783) court painter at Vienna, is painted in the corner spandrel at the front to the right, below the cupola fresco representing the Pentecost miracle. Since early Christian times (Ravenna) pictures of the Evangelists have often been put in the zone between heaven and earth because they carry the divine Word into the world of man. In this picture an angel dictates the text to the evangelist. *Putti* support the bank of clouds which serves as a desk, and hold the sacred book. One of the angel-children has fluttered out of the picture and stands in three-dimensions, on top of the frame; his little body belongs to the tangible world, but his gestures point to the intermediate region of the evangelist. A unique co-operation between painter and stucco worker produced this unbroken transition from heaven to earth.

45. Two *putti* gathering up a curtain. For place, date, and master see Plate 42. The two *putti* crown the top of the altar dedicated to the guardian angels; it stands together with three others at the transversal walls of the crossing. Each of these four altars ends in a rococo scroll; at the back rises an aureole of rays and above this a puffed-out drapery as if the altar were just being unveiled. At all

four altars it is Johann Michael Feichtmayr's angel-children who do this, and we see them here in unparalleled high spirits.

46. *Putto* lifting the edge of a curtain. For place, date, and master see Plate 42. The *putto* is at the left-hand side, next to John the Baptist, the central figure of an altar in the crossing. It is the quietest, relatively, of the altars of the crossing, presumably so as not to disturb the nearby group of the baptism of Christ. Therefore even the curtain-*putto* is quieter than others of his kind. He hides behind the folds rather than opens them, and nestles into the corner behind the palm-leaf, looking dreamingly at the spectator; the very picture of meditation.

47. Two winged angel-heads. For place, date, and master see Plate 42. These two cherubim with *putto*-heads emerge from behind the curtain folds of the guardian angels' altar. The usual purpose of these figures is to indicate the presence of God, as for instance when they appear beside the tabernacle or Holy Ghost's aureole; here, however, they seem to be used as mere decoration, but this is not really so—the two beings turn their gaze straight to heaven, and they remind the spectator of the word of the Lord: "These angels see the face of my Father who is in heaven." They are telling us that the spirits who are appointed to protect us belong, owing to their nature, to the spirits adoring at the throne of God.

48/49. *Putto* with laurel wreath and *putto* with violoncello. In the church of the former Augustinian prebendal abbey at Rottenbuch. The church was originally Gothic, but was supplied with rich rococo decorations by Joseph Schmuzer and his son Franz Xaver between the years 1737 and 1742. To these the sculptor Franz Xaver Schmädl of Weilheim (1705–1777) added between 1740 and 1747 a large high-altar, the effigies of donors, a pulpit, choir-stalls, and an organ-gallery of carved wood. On the choir-stalls there are large figures of David and Aaron, accompanied by a complete choir and orchestra of *putti*-musicians. Not only the words of the psalm "Praise the Lord . . ." are mirrored in these little figures with their well-differentiated movements, but also the preference of the Augustinian canons for figural and orchestral church music, as well as the custom popular in Bavaria and other Alpine countries of praising the Lord with violins, kettle-drums, and trumpets in every village church. The *putti* reproduced here do not belong to this group on the choir-stalls. The *putto* with the wreath accompanies St. Johannes Nepomuk opposite the pulpit; the violinist and the lute player (Plate 25) belong to a quartet in the organ-gallery.

50. Trumpet-blowing *putto*. In the parish church at Isny. Formerly a Benedictine church, it is a simple baroque building in the style of the Vorarlberg churches; in the late fifties of the eighteenth century it was decorated with stucco by Hans Georg Gigl of the Wessobrunn family, later working in the Allgäu. He died in 1765, but was never considered a master of the first rank. The little figure here shows how far the idea of the angel-children had penetrated out to the periphery of contemporary thought.

51. *Putti* embracing each other. In the church of the former Abbey of the Cistercian nuns at Gutenzell in Württemberg. The figures are on the pulpit of the comparatively small convent church and were probably made in about 1763 by Franz Xaver Feichtmayr, a late member of the great stucco-working family. The theme of two *putti* lovingly embracing each other is relatively rare, and was quite unknown in antiquity, for Eros loved the terrestrial girl Psyche, not other *erotes*. Hints at love between *putti* figures can be found on the Sistine vault in Michelangelo's frescoes, but they are lost in the toil and worry of the over-worked children. Michelangelo da Caravaggio painted high on top of his large altar-piece of the seven works of mercy two angels embracing each other, but this looks dangerously sweet. Only towards the end of the era did this minor master succeed

in representing celestial spirits loving each other with child-like naturalness and preaching to us from the pulpit: "Love each other on earth and remember that God on high is Love."

52. *Putto* as charioteer. In the church of the Carmelite monastery Reisach near Rosenheim on the Inn. The simple church of the monastery was the donation of a Bavarian Hofkammerrat (high official in the Finance Department). The court-sculptor Johann Baptist Straub (1704–1784) decorated the interior with wood carvings about 1750. At the side-altar to the right he represented the ascension of the Prophet Elijah, who was supposed to be the protector of the order because of his sojourn on Mount Carmel; for this reason he wears the habit of the order. The representation follows Kings, II, 2, 11, according to which Elijah was taken to heaven in a fiery chariot. Straub, however, added to it a small detail: the chariot-horses are guided with a whip by a *putto*. Accidentally or by design, Pompeian, Roman and late-Baroque *putti* were all occupied in the self-same way.

53. Reading *putti*, 1757. For place and master see Plate 52. The two-angel children sit on the steps of St. Anna's altar. They read the prophesy of the birth of the Virgin and point to the fulfilment of the old hope. The *putti* of the court-sculptor Johann Baptist Straub (1704–1784) a disciple of Raphael Donner, no longer show the liveliness of Johann Michael Feichtmayr's winged children; they are refined and dreamy and their features are more individual.

54. Dance of *putti*. In the Benedictine church of St. Mang in Füssen. This church was given a new form in the Vorarlberg baroque style by the local architect Herkomer; the sculptor Anton Sturm (1690/95–1757), also a native of Füssen, made the figures for the high-altar in marble, and made wood-carvings in the form of a lively circle of dancing *putti* for the pulpit. A dance as motif for

a pulpit decoration had been used already by Donatello in Florence and Prato. The round form of the pulpit in Füssen may have suggested the theme; here it looks as if the sturdy Alpine children were setting a merry-go-round in motion.

55. *Putti* above the miraculous image of Our Lady of Steinbach, 1762. In the pilgrimage church of St. Mary, former succursal church of the Premonstratensian Abbey of Rot on the Rot, now belonging to the Salvatorian Fathers at Maria Steinbach in the Allgäu. After a miraculous apparition of the Virgin the church was built by the Abbey in the years 1746–1753. It seems likely that this country church, in the best style of Upper Swabia, is the work of Dominikus Zimmermann. The artist of the stucco coat was Johann Georg Ueblherr, a skilled master at Wessobrunn (1700–1763) son-in-law of Joseph Schmuzer; he died engaged on this work in 1763. Franz Xaver Feichtmayr finished the decorations. Ueblherr hated symmetry; none of his cornices, none of his picture-frames or his alcoves have two equal parts. His problem was therefore to balance these unequal parts. For choice he used *putti*, setting them in his pictures as weights to restore the balance where they were needed. They always seem to move to the spots where one part is threatening to be disconnected or to plunge down. This applies not only to single details of the architecture, but to the building as a whole; Ueblherr never saw an altar, a pulpit, a balcony or a gallery by itself; he always saw an undulating whole, and the *putti* swing themselves as if on a trapeze from one end of it to the other.

56. *Putto* playing with a curtain. In the chapel of St. Anastasia, an oval Rococo addition to the monks' choir in the church of the former Benedictine Monastery at Benedictbeuren. It was built by Johann Michael Fischer; the paintings are by Zeiller and Amigoni, and there are three altars from the workshop of Ignaz Günther (1725–1775), which were set up in 1753. The *putto* shown here lies on the architrave of the side-altar to the left. In contrast to the curtain-gathering *putto*

mentioned above, he is unoccupied and is playing hide and seek with the spectator. He has just lifted the curtain, in a moment he will let it drop and make himself invisible. This is the coquetry of a child, sweet and charming, but no more a ritual play; it is "heavenly" playfulness.

57. Two little angel-heads, 1762. For place and master see Plate 55. They are two cherubim angels, calling out to each other on the architrave of the side-altar to the left.

58–59. *Putto* with flower garland in the dusk, and small angels holding a candle-stick. For place and master see Plate 55. All Ueblherr *putti* are brothers; all look out of deep-set, almost almond-shaped eyes, all have the same large mouth open as if to shout. Are they all Ueblherr's own children?

60. *Putto* with book and lamb, 1756. In the church of the former Premonstratensian, now Benedictine Abbey of Schäftlarn. The church was built according to plans by Cuvilliés, Gunetsrhainer and Johann Michael Fischer; the court-sculptor in Munich, Johann Baptist Straub, 1704–1784, decorated it. He crowned the tabernacle with the Lamb of Revelation and the Book of the Seven Seals; at its side emerges a *putto* carved in wood and gilded. His small left hand is lifted and shades the happy and triumphant face and the mouth opening to sing praises: "Worthy is the Lamb that was slain to receive power and riches and wisdom and strength . . ."

61. Adoring *putto*. In the former Premonstratensian church of Neustift-Freising, rebuilt after a fire by Johann Michael Fischer, and equipped in 1756-1757 by Ignaz Günther (1725–1775) with the high-altar, choir-stalls and the Eastern pair of side-altars, on the first of which is the kneeling *putto* (made of wood and alabaster, partly painted and gilded). It is usually admitted that this last of the great Bavarian Rococo sculptors possessed "the aesthetic charm of perfect lines

and the sensual charm of overt feeling", but "that one misses in him the deep and warm quality which still distinguished the masters of the generation of 1690." This *putto* proves that that is too sweeping a judgment. The adoring angel-child, approaching the age of an ephebe, makes a perfect whole with his outline; his movements reveal deep feelings, his expression shows that he is quite oblivious of himself, absorbed in events which are invisible, yet the centre of these must be in his own breast, which he protects with his folded hands; it is the mysticism of childhood.

62/63/64. *Putto* in an aureole, *putti* with cartouche, and another *putto* with cartouche. In the former Augustinian Prebendal church at Weyarn, an early Baroque building, for which Ignaz Günther (1725–1775) carved in 1755 the tabernacle of the high-altar. He also made groups with the Virgin, as well as a southern and a northern side-altar: these are called *putti*-altars because of their angel-aureoles. One must admit that the service the *putti* performs is partly a mere pretext. The cartouches show neither writing nor emblems, they simply belong to the equipment of the *putti*. These little figures are placed there so that one should fall in love with them. If for their sake we too become as little children there is, according to the word of the Lord, some hope that we may enter the kingdom of heaven. Ignaz Günther made mainly two kinds of *putti*: a clumsy coquettish one, verging on the sweet and sentimental (Plates 62, 64) and a more sturdy, rustic one with red cheeks, who, though a little girlish, is full of energy when he strides out or seizes hold of things (Plate 63). The latter type has more vital energy. The master himself and his disciple Götsch went on making this type in Rott on the Inn.

65. *Putto* holding the canopy of a throne. In the church of the former Premonstratensian Abbey at Rot on the Rot in Württemberg. The stucco decoration

of this church, the joint work of Franz Xaver Feichtmayr and his brother Simpert, already shows features of the Classical Revival. The *putto* here (1774) is ascribed to Franz Xaver Feichtmayr II. It is a calm figure, receding behind the folds of the canopy rather than turning it back or raising it; the *putto's* eyes glance downwards, the first sign of farewell.

66/67/68. *Putto* with palm and laurel-wreath, *Putto* with book, *Putto* with cardinal's hat. In the church of the former Benedictine Abbey at Rott on the Inn. The church is a late work of Johann Michael Fischer and was decorated with the late work of Ignaz Günther in 1762 and by his disciple Joseph Götsch in 1763. The three *putti* reproduced here are little attribute-angels. They should really be showing the attributes of their masters to the spectator. However, in Rott this aim has been forgotten. The *putto* next to St. Ambrosius balances a laurel-wreath and palm; this would have been the correct attribute for a holy martyr, but St. Ambrosius was no martyr. The *putto* beside St. Augustine carries a book, but the attribute of this holy Father of the church ought to have been either a shell filled with water or a heart. Finally the *putto* above St. Petrus Damianus indulges in a rather daring joke, for he has taken possession of the cardinal's hat. Even the placing of the *putti* is unusual. The *putti* next to St. Ambrosius and St. Damianus do not stand as mediators between the figures of the saints and the spectator, but are placed high above the former. Nor do they merge with the frames of the picture, they seem to have arrived by flying. And it appears especially grotesque that a cherub should serve as loincloth to the *putto* of St. Ambrosius! All this represents a dissolution of the old order, though it increased the individual charm of the little figures—they are indeed playing about with the old order. This is most evident when one looks at the *putto* who with cheeky charm puts the cardinal's hat on his own head. With the features of the young Voltaire this would have been blasphemy, but that Bavarian urchin—no, it is impossible to be angry with him, nor with another one, who carries the sacred book not in the least like a ministrant, but offers it more as a little waiter would offer a specially fragrant dish. All three make us smile ironically; yet there is also some sadness, for one feels that the art is on the verge of decadence.

69. *Putti* adoring the holy Sacrament. Top of a cupboard in the sacristy of the Benedictine basilica at Ettal. The artist is unknown; we assume that the group, in an early Rococo style, dates from about 1720, one generation before the *putti* in Rott on the Inn. Composition and movement show less genius than in Günther's figures, but it is pleasant here to find everything still in its right place: the little head of the cherub is the throne of the Lord in the Sacrament; the *putto* to the left folds his hands with child-like innocence before the chalice of salvation, and the *putto* to the right invites the spectator to do so too. Simple symmetry produces the solemnity of the High Mass familiar to the Bavarian peasants.

70. Retreating *putto*, 1748. In the pilgrimage church of St. Mary, Beloved Mother, in Birnau. The building was commissioned by the Cistercian Abbey at Salem. The church, which gives us a fore-taste of the approaching classicism, was erected between 1745 and 1755 by the architect Peter Thumb, with the help of the sculptor Joseph Anton Feuchtmayer (1696–1770) and his assistant Johann Georg Dirr (1723–1790). The *putto* reproduced here leans against John the Baptist's altar, the side-altar to the left in the chancel. He is made in flesh-coloured stucco, a work by Joseph Anton Feuchtmayer. The altar is asymmetrical, built as a spiral of which the *putto* forms the base. The *putto* shows that it is a spiral going down not upwards, for he has to set his legs wide apart so as not to slide down, and his features reflect his terror of the depth. The angle at which his right leg is stretched

out is common to many of Joseph Anton Feuchtmayer's *putti*; it is an effective diagonal, but ties the figure to the ground.

71. The so-called honey-licker. For place, date and master see Plate 70. The *putto* stands at the altar of St. Bernard, the founder of the Cistercian order, who since the Middle Ages has been called Doctor Mellifluus, the teacher from whom honey flows. The *putto* symbolises this title. St. Bernard's altar too avoids symmetry, and so the *putto* stands to the left of the altar on a volute without any counterpart, almost like a monumental free-standing sculpture. His superiority to other *putti* with regard to the balance of movement, the assurance with which his body is formed and the significance of his expression have made him the most famous *putto* in Germany. The theme invites comparisons: in the hands of Ignaz Günther it might have been used for a doubtful joke; but in Birnau there is no place for levity; the boy explores seriously the taste of the honey, that is to say St. Bernard's teaching.

72. *Putto* with legend of the consecration of the church, 1750. For place and master see Plate 70. This *putto* by Feuchtmayer is placed under the organ-gallery. The banderol announces: "Haec ecclesia constructa est anno MDCCL" (this church was built in 1750). The mannered and slim body of the child hangs rather than hovers in a surrealist and bizarre sky; he does not hold the banderol, but seems held by it. The little boy, his figure detached from the background, and set alone in a wide oval, is made in pale flesh coloured stucco.

73. Group of *putti* with palm branch, 1749. For place and master see Plate 70. This pair of *putti* is placed above the archivolt to the right of the high-altar. The triangular composition rises skilfully to the top of the palm branch—but cannot conceal the effort of this triumph. It is the function of the reclining *putto* to symbolise the mighty difficulties which have to be overcome to reach the top.

71

The other *putto*, standing upright, looks carefully downwards and sideways; is the palm really his? The stucco is of alabaster-colour, with gilded palm and wings.

74. *Putto* with chalice, 1757; for place and master see Plate 70. As in many pilgrimage churches there is in Birnau a gallery all round the interior. Joseph Anton Feuchtmayer and his disciple and assistant Johann Georg Dirr (1723–1779) have placed on it the figures of the apostles, carved in wood and gilded; to each of them they added a *putto*. The *putto* with the chalice reproduced here is placed beside St. John the Evangelist. It is the work of Johann Georg Dirr.

75. Pair of *putti* with chalice, cross and book, 1750. For place and master see Plate 70. These *putti* on the roof of the pulpit are the work of Feuchtmayer. The theme had been popular since the Council of Trent; like a sermon, it was concerned with the chief truths of the Christian faith: the Incarnation and Salvation (the cross), the Holy Sacraments (the chalice), and the Last Judgment (the Lamb of Revelation). Here too the composition rises from a broad base laboriously but logically, while a shadow falls from above over the faces of the children, who look very serious.

76. *Putto* playing the lute. In the church of the former Cistercian Abbey at Salem. A Gothic building, provided in about 1766 with a richly ornamented organ and organ-gallery; the decorations are of wood and stucco, and are to be attributed to Johann Georg Dirr (1723–1779), a disciple of Joseph Anton Feuchtmayer, with whom he also worked at Birnau. In the years 1774–1794 a completely new piece of decoration was added in the form of a very large picture high behind the altar, 26 side-altars, balustrades etc., all in white and pale pink alabaster with grey veining. The work was done by Johann George Dirr until his death in 1779, and then carried on by his son-in-law Johann Georg Wieland. Johann Georg Dirr put the last musician-*putto* of the dying Baroque on to the

organ gallery about 1766. The little troubadour's movements are still freely and generously conceived, but the expression of his face is not only sad, he also looks terribly ill.

77. *Putto* with jug and cloth; for place and master see Plate 76. In 1774–1779 Johann Georg Dirr made for the triangular chancel screens in front of the high-altar pairs of *putti* with the instruments of the Passion or with other things connected with it. This group here points to the words of Pilate: "I will wash my hands of it." The elongated groups in precious alabaster appear to rise, but if one looks at the bodies separately, one notices that they are not rising but sinking down, as it were a refined pining away.

78/79. *Putti* climbing up a palm. For place, date, and master see Plate 76. The palm stands on the organ-gallery and was therefore made about ten years before the alabaster decoration of the nave. The material is still wood and stucco, richly painted in flesh tints, red, blue and gold. The angel-children make preparations for a feast and try to fasten a garland with ribbons and wreaths to the top of the palm tree. It is a late Baroque joke, the composition most successful—but none of the *putti* smiles.

80. *Putti* holding a platter with John the Baptist's head upon it, 1774–1779; for place and master, see Plate 76. The whole of the high-altar at Salem is made to look like a huge sarcophagus. This graveyard mood has spread throughout the church's interior, even over the socle of the altar and the platter with John's head represented there. Copies of the platter in which Herodias had carried the Baptist's head were greatly venerated in the late Middle Ages; in the Baroque era the veneration only survived locally. Here the conception was taken up again as a symbol of the death of sanctity. The well-formed *putti* bow humbly before their own fate and death.

ACKNOWLEDGMENTS

The author and the publishers wish to thank all those who helped with the publication of this book by putting photographs etc., at their disposal and by kindly giving permission for reproductions.

The originals of the pictures reproduced here are in the following collections:

Plate 1: Museum of Antiquities in Munich;

Plate 5: Verlag Urachhaus in Stuttgart;

Plate 18 and the Dürer drawings interspersed in the text: "Graphische Sammlung" in Munich;

Plate 19: Bavarian Landesamt für Denkmalpflege in Munich;

Plate 22: Bildarchiv Sepp Rostra in Augsburg;

Plate 25: H. Kronburger, Oberammergau;

Plates 16, 23, 24, and 28–80 are the German publisher's reproductions made with Linhof-Technica 9 by 12; those of them which are in colour with Agfa-color CT.B.9, Leica; all others are from the archives of the German publisher.

Bowl by the Telephos painter, *c.* 460 B.C.

Roman sarcophagus of the 4th century

Roman relief, 3rd-4th centuries

Sarcophagus, 2nd century

Eros and Psyche, early 3rd century

Burial urn from the time of Hadrian

Small bronze from Pompeii, *c.* A.D. 50

Domitilla catacomb, *c.* A.D. 200

Roman sarcophagus, 3rd century

9

Mosaic floor in the Aquileia Basilica, *c*. A.D. 320

Mosaic floor in the Aquileia Basilica, *c.* A.D. 320

Agostino d'Antonio di Duccio (1418-98)

Donatello (1386–1466)

Raffaello Santi (1483–1520)

Raffaelo Santi (1483–1520)

Wood relief in St. Giustina in Padua, *c.* 1560

Michelangelo Buonarroti (1475–1564)

Albrecht Dürer (1471–1528)

Ascribed to Georg Petel (1590–1633)

Raymond de la Fage (1656-90)

Sebastian Loscher, who worked in Augsburg between 1510–48

Franz Xaver Schmädl (1705–77)

Johann Baptist Straub (1704–84)

Franz Xaver Schmädl (1705 - 1777)

Pompeji, 1. Jhdt. v. Chr.

Pompeji, 1. Jhdt. v. Chr.

lrremur. P eundē cc.

C In die sancti pa-
tris nostri Augustini
episcopi Introitus

Posch-Missale, 1526

Posch-Missale, 1526

29

Christoph Rodt (1575/1580-1634)

Dominikus Zimmermann (1685 - 1766)

Ägid Quirin Asam (1692-1750)

Ägid Quirin Asam (1692-1750)

Ägid Quirin Asam (1692–1750)

Ägid Quirin Asam (1692 - 1750)

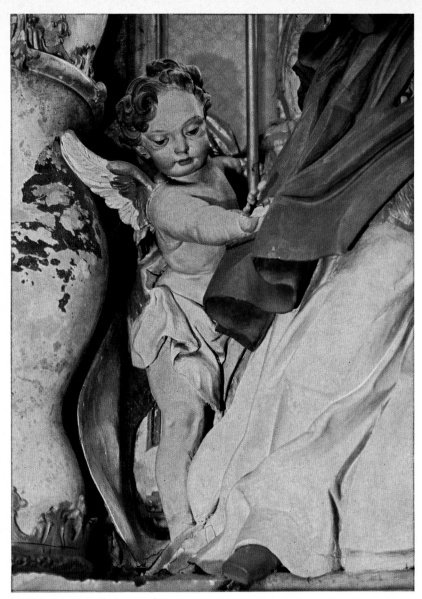

Ägid Quirin Asam (1692-1750)

Ignaz Günther (1725 - 1775)

Johann Michael Feichtmayr (1709-1772)

Johann Michael Feichtmayr (1709-1772)

Johann Michael Feichtmayr (1709 - 1772)

Johann Michael Feichtmayr (1709-1772)

Johann Michael Feichtmayr (1709-1772)

Johann Michael Feichtmayr (1709-1772)

Johann Jakob Zeiller (1710-1783)

44

Johann Michael Feichtmayr (1709-1772)

Johann Michael Feichtmayr (1709-1772)

Johann Michael Feichtmayr (1709-1772)

Franz Xaver Schmädl (1705 - 1777)

Franz Xaver Schmädl (1705-1777)

Hans Georg Gigl († 1765)

Franz Xaver Feichtmayr

Johann Baptist Straub (1704-1784)

Johann Baptist Straub (1704-1784)

Anton Sturm (1690/95 - 1757)

Johann Georg Üblherr (1700‑1763)

Ignaz Günther (1725-1775)

Johann Georg Üblherr (1700-1763)

Johann Georg Üblherr (1700-1763)

Johann Georg Üblherr (1700-1763)

Johann B. Straub (1704-1784)

Ignaz Günther (1725 - 1775)

Ignaz Günther (1725-1775)

Ignaz Günther (1725 - 1775)

Ignaz Günther (1725 - 1775)

Franz Xaver Feichtmayr II, dates from 1774

Joseph Götsch, dates from 1763

Joseph Götsch, dates from 1763

Ignaz Günther (1725 - 1775)

Early rococo (about 1720)

Joseph Anton Feuchtmayer (1696-1770)

Joseph Anton Feuchtmayer (1696-1770)

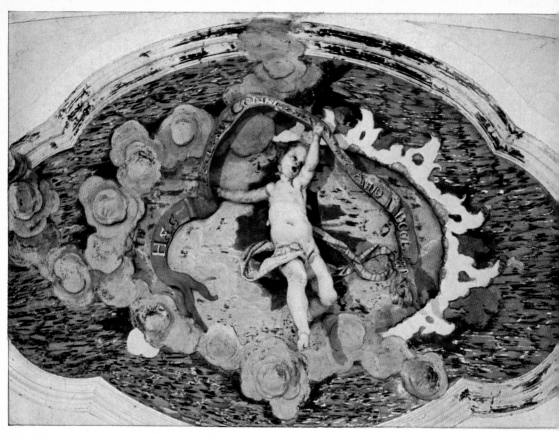

Joseph Anton Feuchtmayer (1696 - 1770)

Joseph Anton Feuchtmayer (1696-1770)

Johann Georg Dirr (1723-1779)

Joseph Anton Feuchtmayer (1696-1770)

Johann Georg Dirr (1723-1779)

Johann Georg Dirr (1723-1779)

Johann Georg Dirr (1723-1779)

Johann Georg Dirr (1723-1779)

Johann Georg Dirr (1723-1779)